ALSO BY CHRISENA COLEMAN

Mama Knows Best:
African-American Wives' Tales, Myths,
and Remedies for Mothers and Mothers-to-Be

Just
Between
Girlfriends

African-American Women
Celebrate Friendship

CHRISENA COLEMAN

SIMON & SCHUSTER

SIMON & SCHUSTER
Rockefeller Center
1230 Avenue of the Americas
New York, NY 10020

SIMON & SCHUSTER and colophon are registered trademarks of
Simon & Schuster Inc.

Designed by Ruth Lee

Manufactured in the United States of America

3   5   7   9   10   8   6   4   2

Library of Congress Cataloging-in-Publication Data
Coleman, Chrisena.
Just between girlfriends : African-American women
celebrate friendship / Chrisena Coleman.
p.   cm.
1. Female friendship—Anecdotes. 2. Afro-American
women—Psychology—Anecdotes. I. Title.
BF575.F66C64   1998
302.3'4—dc21   98-3201
CIP

ISBN 0-684-84676-4

THIS BOOK IS DEDICATED TO

My best friend in the whole wide world, Linda Taylor. Thank you so very much for believing in me and encouraging me to reach for the stars, no matter how difficult things appeared. Remember how you used to cut out my tiny little newspaper articles and hang them on the refrigerator with T.J., Tanisha, and Paula's artwork? Well, make room on the refrigerator—here's another book cover to hang up. We've become closer than girlfriends—you are the sister I always dreamed about. *Luv you!*

My childhood friends, Kathy Clay-Boyd and Cynthia Nadine Wooden. Wow! We've certainly come a long way since our journey began—playing kick ball on Third Street. Remember Miss Claudie, Hey Bebop, Happy Jack, Grandpop (sitting in his favorite chair watching television), Carrot-Top and Twinkle-Toes? And how can we forget those yellow jackets, the Rambler, the Family Wagon, doing my laundry, and the day Baby Shyra came home from the hospital.

Though it was your older sisters, Sheila Clay-Coles and Linda Wooden, who really brought us together, it was our sense of adventure, strong family ties, and a loving spirit that kept us intact. I'm thankful for our mothers, Dorothy Coleman (Dot), Esther Clay (88), and Loretta Wooden (Lu-Lu), who reminded us how ridiculous we were each time we stopped speaking to each other over something petty and helped us blossom into the wonderful women we are today. *Friends 'til the end!*

Acknowledgments

Thanks to all the women who shared their stories with me. An extra special thanks to my parents, Wilbert and Dorothy Coleman (the world's greatest); my brother, Mustafa (thanks for letting me kidnap you; I couldn't have finished this book without you, "Uncle"); and thanks to the rest of the family for their support. Jordan Christopher, mommy loves you. Eric, your support amazes me. Thanks to Rev. Gregory Jackson, his wife, Barbara, and the Mt. Olive Church Family. A special thank you to Mrs. Thelma Smith, principal of Nellie K. Parker Elementary School (Hackensack, N.J.), and her wonderful staff! Another thanks to my mentor, Jerry Schmetterer, who always encourages me to "go for it!"

Thank you, Laurie Chittenden (my new editor)—it's been a pleasure working with you. The next one will be even more fun. Annie Hughes-O'Connor (my former editor)—I miss you and I know you miss me singing all the time. Eileen (my Arliss) Cope, of Lowenstein-Morel & Associates, thanks for everything.

*   *   *

I'm extremely blessed to have made some beautiful friends over the years. Shelley Worrell (my ace), who understands and supports me. Veronica Joyner, who should have been a therapist. Denene Millner and Adrienne Rhodes, who help me get over hurdles at the *Daily News*. Adriane Gaines, Sandra Harper, Loretta Braddy, Evelyn Cunningham, Carrie Pearson, Rahda Smith, and Brenda Blackmon, who I consider my mature girlfriends. Angelita, who keeps me competitive. Then there's Joyce Gillespie, who is my West Coast connection. Paula Reece (a.k.a. Mama Montego). Charise Reid, who keeps it real. Pat Battle, who keeps me awake on New Jersey assignments. Tonya Stewart, Kim Lynch, Judy Hutson, Tonya Ramey, Ruthie Thomas, and Terrie Williams. Holly Alston, Gwynne Marshall, Madeline Carrino, Sister Jackie, Rae Brown, and the Rev. Suzan Johnson Cook, who pray with me and for me—*Say Amen Somebody*. Carol Ann Campbell, Dayna Bottazzi, Karen Lombardi, Lisa Guzman, Cheri Martino, Molly Gordy, Andrea Graham, Linda Stasi, and Amy Pagnozzi, who can honestly tell people "one of my closest friends is black." Natalie, Felecia, Lesvia, Karen, Sandra, Stacy, Pamela, Kipper, Rachel, and Robyn—the mommy club. And of course, my neighbor and new friend, Crystal, who doesn't have a choice in the matter.

With all these names, it's obvious why I am writing a book about friendship. Through the laughter, pain, shame, joy, confusion, and times of trouble, these girlfriends have been there for me and I've been there for them, too. They have played detective when I was suspicious about an unfaithful boyfriend. They have defended my name when someone criticized me behind my back. And they love me, despite my moods, strong opinions, and deadlines.

All women, especially African-American women, need girlfriends. My friendship with these women knows no boundaries. The ties that bind us together will remain tightly secured forever.

In God We Trust

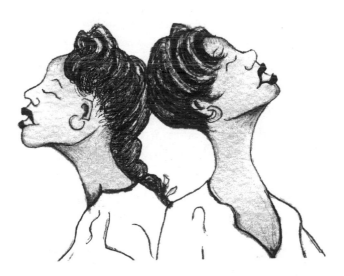

Contents

Introduction

Thank God for girlfriends! Who else would try so hard to keep our secrets, laugh hysterically at our silly jokes, wipe our tears after yet another breakup, take us out to celebrate our engagement (or divorce for that matter), and stand by our side as we make our way through all the trials and tribulations that life has to offer?

Only a true friend.

Girlfriends. They will go out of their way for you, because they know you would do the same. So it's okay to pick up the phone and call them at the last minute to babysit, or borrow a few bucks, as long as you do it for them when they are in a pinch. And when they call you in the middle of the night laughing and giggling after a great date, you must get excited too, no matter how tired you are. Girlfriends will stop what they're doing and give you their undivided attention, even when they should be working, paying closer attention to their children, or spending time with their man. And in times of real trouble, they will drop everything in order to support you. Even when we put our girlfriends on a shelf, only to call or see them once in a while, they'll understand because they know they can expect the same from us. Go ahead—share your secrets with them because you know they will keep these close to their heart.

As we travel down life's highway, venturing off to college or the workforce, marriage, motherhood (not necessarily in that order), divorce, sickness, and even death, we gather new friends and occasionally lose a few along the way.

Though it's hard to admit, no one is perfect. We all make mistakes and we all do things that may annoy and disappoint our friends on occasion. I can remember quite a few times when my friends left me wondering if they did indeed have my best interest at heart. And I know that I have disappointed my friends at times, too, but I believe God sends special people our way for a reason.

As we celebrate the beauty, loyalty, and love of our girlfriends, it's important for us to agree to disagree at times, have patience, and accept the fact that our girlfriends may not always be as sensitive, considerate, or loving as we'd like them to be. But no matter what, they *are* still our girlfriends, so we must try our best to understand.

The ties that bind friends are the deepest and strongest of all. Girlfriends are carefully selected—and we often demand more of them than others and maybe even ourselves. We choose our girlfriends because we see special qualities in them that we admire, appreciate, and perhaps either wish for or even see in ourselves.

So what if you don't like her husband, or her children, for

that matter. That's okay. You picked your girlfriend because of the wonderful qualities *she* possesses. If you're an AKA (like me—*skee-wee*), it's okay that your best friend is a Delta, Zeta, or Sigma Gamma Rho—the names of the organizations are different, but the purpose to promote and help women is the same. You may be a Democrat and your girlfriend is a Republican—that's okay, too. Girlfriends come from many different circles of life: We meet them through work, church, the neighborhood, college, our children, husbands or boyfriends, aerobics, shopping, Friday night Spades and Bid Whist, Pokeno, and almost everyone has one or two lifelong friends like my childhood friends, Kathy and Cindy.

Our girlfriends know all about our problems: cranky kids, weight fluctuations, racist bosses, contractors from hell, good and bad dates, marital problems, health problems, accomplishments, sorrows, promotions, demotions, insecurities, leaky faucets, and very often they know of our news before we tell them. Our girlfriends have a way of sensing things.

Yet, despite our best intentions, many of us are too busy trying to be mother of the year, corporate executive, perfect wife, loving fiancée, or whatever it is—to give our girlfriends the attention they deserve. We often tend to lose sight of just how important our girlfriends are—and that is why I am writing *Just Between Girlfriends*.

I hope this book will make you pick up the telephone and call your girlfriends, one by one. Round them up and tell them it's time for a reunion or a girlfriends' night out. Rekindle the special relationship you once shared or still do with friends new and old. *Just Between Girlfriends* is a gentle reminder of the importance of girlfriends. By sharing inspirational, heartwarming, and funny anecdotes I have collected from African-American women across the country, I hope you will be inspired to reach out for your girlfriends. I have spoken to women—old, young, and in between—who have told me candid, graceful, and delightful stories about the special friendships that have shaped and touched their lives. The most special ones I collected are contained in this book as a celebration and inspiration to women. Thank God for our girlfriends—no matter where they may be.

My Own First Friends

WHILE SOME OF YOU MAY HAVE TO THINK BACK A LITTLE FUR-
ther than others, I'm sure you all have fond memories of your
very first friend. You know the one you promised to remain
close to until death do you part. I remember making that
pledge to my very first friend, Kathy Clay. We met in kindergarten, in September of 1968. Her mother let her bring a doll
to school and my mom didn't, so I stole hers while the rest of
the class was napping, simply because I was jealous. It was a
little blond-haired doll dressed in a yellow rain slicker.

When my dad picked me up from school that day, the
teacher told him that Kathy's doll was missing and I was the
last one who played with it. Actually, I'd hidden the doll because I didn't have one at school. We ended up at Woolworth,
searching for a replacement doll. I pretended that I couldn't
remember what Kathy's doll looked like, so I selected a dark
brown–skinned doll, with short, kinky black hair (too young
to realize that black is beautiful) and we delivered it to her
house.

Prior to going to school, Kathy and I had never met,
though we lived only a few blocks away from each other. To
my surprise, Kathy's mother and my parents had known
each other for years. Then again, because my dad was one of
a few black police officers on the Hackensack Police Force in
the 1960s, everyone seemed to know us. When we arrived at
Kathy's house with the new doll, my father apologized pro-

fusely for my behavior and explained to Miss Clay that he did not raise me to steal.

When I forked the doll over to Kathy, I licked my tongue at her on the sly and mumbled, "I'm sorry."

Yet the very next day at school, Kathy and I stood next to each other during the flag salute, sat next to each other at snack time, and lay side by side at nap time. I never did tell her where I hid the doll, and for some reason, Kathy forgave me. At 5 years old Kathy already seemed to understand and accept that sometimes friends disappoint each other. In fact, from that day on, we were inseparable.

At Fanny Hillers Elementary School we walked home together, every day leaving our tracks all over the perfectly manicured lawns we passed through. Though we were not in the same classes, every year we made a point of spending time together before and after school.

At Hackensack Middle School, Kathy and I met a new best friend, Cindy Wooden, and we quickly became the three musketeers—the black version of Charlie's Angels (with a head full of wildly thick hair, of course, I was Farrah—or so I thought). We wore the same clothes, talked on the telephone all night, chased boys, went to parties, shared secrets, argued with each other, played "the dozens," and cosigned each other's lies when we wanted to "get over" on our parents. We had become so close that our families became one, slept over regularly, and as young girls struggled to understand why Cindy's father (who Kathy and I affectionately called Uncle Frank) died of cancer at such an early age.

We giggled together and seemed to get in trouble far too frequently during classes. Like the day I turned around and flashed a big gummy smile after I had twisted two long braids on each side of my head, which sent Kathy and Cindy into hysterics. We disrupted the class and drove poor Mrs. Korczenski nutty. Or the countless times Mr. Schott embarrassed me in front of the whole class by threatening to call my mother to tell her how I'd misbehaved so that she'd rip my teen-line phone out of the wall, as she promised to do if I were unruly in class. "Don't let me call Dot," he would say. Again, Kathy and Cindy howled because they knew my mom really would rip that phone out in a heartbeat.

And I have to admit, we had our share of catty times too, like all the *he said, she said* arguments we waged and the many battles to be the other's best, best friend—as if having two best friends were not possible. We talked behind each other's back and lied about it when confronted. But in the end, we always managed to work out our differences and we learned to overlook the slips in loyalty. We were, after all, best friends.

In high school, we jumped out of a second-floor window at Hackensack High School in order to hang out with the older boys we tried so hard to impress. Later, when we were caught by Mr. Capone and sentenced to detention, we didn't care as long as we were together. It was then that I confessed to Kathy that in kindergarten I had thrown her doll inside the top of the piano. She busted out laughing and marveled at how many years our friendship had lasted through thick and thin. Kathy and Cindy were right by my side the day an older girl and I duked it out after school, each time the red-headed boy I thought I loved put me down for another girl, and every time my parents grounded me. We were together at every "blue-light-in-the-basement party," drank our first sips of "shorty," smoked our first and last cigarette together, and toked our first spliff together. And when school officials canceled our senior pep rally, we helped galvanize the seniors by arranging for someone to pull the fire alarm. When it sounded, we all marched out of class and into the streets for an unofficial pep rally.

After high school, we each went our separate ways—I went off to college in Boston, Kathy went to college in Washington, D.C., and Cindy took on a full-time job. We met up every holiday and summer, sharing episodes from our different lives and creating new memories for the three of us. Like Cindy's father taking us crabbing, Kathy's mother's spider-heeled shoes, and the night my mom discovered that her 17-year-old daughter was drunk instead of having a bad case of food poisoning.

Though we don't see or talk to each other every day or every week, like we did when we were kids, we are still good friends today. In fact, Kathy's daughter, Kelsey, and my son, Jordan, are playmates. Now we're anxiously waiting for Cindy to become a mommy.

The many memories shared by Kathy, Cindy, and I make us laugh, cry, and reflect upon the bond we have created over the years. It is so refreshing to get together some 25 years later to reminisce about the good old days, though they seem like only yesterday. Sure, we each have new friends and maybe even closer friends, but we share a special bond that will keep us dear friends till the end. Our memories will never fade, for they remain etched in our hearts. It was the values, lessons, and adventures we found as the three musketeers—and our very first friends—that set the stage for our new friendships to follow. We grow and learn and inevitably make mistakes along the way, but it is our very first friendships—the innocence, loyalty, and honesty—that will always remind us of what we expect from friends throughout our lives.

As I wrote about Kathy and Cindy, I found myself pulling out old photo albums, letters, and even our Hackensack High School Class of 1981 yearbook. I sat there smiling and at times even laughing out loud as I flipped through the pages containing the moments of our lives. My memories about Kathy and Cindy prompted me to ask other women about their very first friend.

As I reflected on my own experience, I was not surprised that everyone I spoke to also smiled when they remembered their first friend. Many recalled childhood games such as Double-Dutch, Jacks, Punchanella, and Hopscotch. And who could forget the many hand games such as Miss Mary Mack, Mack, Mack! We didn't know it back then, but these were games that truly separated the girls from the boys; they were games that girls played. Now I'm sharing these stories with you and I am sure you'll smile too.

Who knows? Maybe this chapter is just the boost you need to pick up the phone and try to reach out to one of your childhood girlfriends. Good luck and happy memories.

Make That Two Orders of
Chicken Pox, Please!

Jill and Sandy were next-door neighbors and quickly became inseparable. Whenever you saw one, you saw the other, like two peas in a pod. They played with dolls, collected comic books, and often wore the same outfits, as if they were twins. One day Jill called Sandy to say she wouldn't be in school because she had come down with a bad case of chicken pox. Sandy hung up the phone and reluctantly went to school. She missed Jill terribly. In fact, on the way home from school Sandy stopped by to visit Jill, hoping she too would come down with the chicken pox.

Guess what? It worked! The friends spent the next couple of days in Jill's bedroom massaging their pox with calamine lotion and trying not to scratch. Sure they were uncomfortable, but neither one cared as long as they were together.

Talky-Talky

Ten-year-old Britney Vanessa McCoy said her best friend is a girl in her class named Jen. She describes Jen as funny, generous, kind, and she plays a mean game of kickball.

"I love to talk," Britney confessed. "In fact, I talk all the time. If I am not talking, then I am usually asleep. My friend Jen is quiet and seldom says a word. Some people wonder why we like to be together because we're so different, but that's what makes our friendship work. When I think about it, if Jen talked as much as I do, we probably wouldn't be friends. Who would be there to listen to me?"

Do You Have a Daughter?

As Shelley rode up and down her new suburban street in the back seat of her mother's station wagon, she spotted a little girl who looked just about her age. Then one day, Shelley decided to venture down her block to find out more about the little girl. When she reached the house, Shelley saw a woman standing outside.

"Do you have a daughter?" Shelley asked.

"Yes, I do," the woman replied. "Her name is Lisa."

"Can I play with her?" Shelley asked.

"Of course you can," the woman answered.

Shelley and Lisa quickly became best friends. They played dolls on the porch, school in the backyard, and went to summer camp together. And whenever Lisa's mom cooked fried chicken, the two girls would come up with a scheme for Shelley to eat over.

They remained friends over the years. Though they are both grown up and have families of their own, Lisa still invites Shelley over for some of her mother's Southern fried chicken whenever she's in town.

Giggles and Boogies

Crystal had seen Charmaine at school, but they never said much to each other. Then one day, Charmaine walked Crystal home and said she wanted to become her friend.

"When we got to my mother's house, Charmaine and I sat on the porch talking about our second-grade teachers," Crystal recalled.

Though they stayed outside for some time, Crystal wasn't quite sure if she wanted to be pals with Charmaine. But the defining moment came when Charmaine blurted out one of the silliest questions Crystal had ever heard: "Don't you like digging up your nose and playing with your boogers?"

"I looked at her and started laughing," Crystal said. "It was so funny to me. Then Charmaine laughed, too! We couldn't stop laughing—in fact, we still laugh about it to this day."

Lost & Found

Betty Thompson was my mother's first friend. They met on the stoop of their Harlem apartment building, in 1937. My mom remembered that she and Betty were drawn to each other because they lived in the same St. Nicholas Terrace building, were the same age, both had older sisters, and they also had a head full of long black hair.

"Neither one of us liked to get our hair done," Mom recalled. "We'd rather stay outside and play."

Their friendship flourished over the years. My mother

eventually married and moved from Harlem to Hackensack, New Jersey, and met a whole new set of friends. She often thought about Betty, but never tried to locate her. Then, nearly 45 years after they had met on St. Nicholas Terrace, my mother and Betty ran into each other in a mall in New Jersey. I was with my mom that day and I still remember the sparkle in her eye when she and Betty recognized each other.

They both still had beautiful thick hair and marveled at how nice the other's hair looked. They talked about the old neighborhood and tried to fill in the missing years. Mom and Betty exchanged numbers and vowed to stay in touch. Over the next 10 years, they exchanged Christmas cards, telephone calls, and even had dinner a few times. My mother was always excited when she heard from Betty; she was a link to the past.

Then one day, another friend of Betty's called my mother to tell her that Betty had passed on. My mom sat on the edge of her bed for a long time, saddened because her first friend had died, knowing that Betty's death had closed a chapter in her own book of life.

Thanks, Mom & Dad

When Tonja Ward thinks about her very first friend, a cute little picture of Keisha Jackson instantly appears. "I don't know when I met her, but it seems like we've been friends forever," Tonja told me. "We met at church. Our parents were friends, so they kinda pushed us together."

Though children often think parents are not good at selecting their friends, Tonja still thanks her parents for Keisha. As youngsters growing up in Atlanta, they went to church and school together. The girls never got hassled by their parents when they asked to visit each other or to go out together.

"Keisha and I had a lot of good times together," Tonja said. "I loved her honesty, openness, and willingness to help others."

Tonja and Keisha don't speak to each other regularly, but they are still close friends. "We are the kind of friends who can always pick up exactly where we left off," said Tonja. "That's what makes our friendship so special."

Seeing Double

Leslie was all decked out in her blue, black, and gray plaid Catholic school jumper with matching beret when she walked outside her apartment building and discovered there was another little girl wearing the very same uniform. She told Leslie her name was Iovanna and Leslie flashed an approving smile. Then Iovanna's grandmother asked Leslie's father if she could give them a ride to school. At school the girls were in the same class and that was just the beginning of a lifelong friendship.

In the Mirror

Janelle laughs when she tells the story, but she was her own first friend. The youngest of four children and the only girl in the house, little Janelle's brothers would not let her play with them.

As she walked by a full-body mirror in the hallway of her apartment one day, she expressed her desire to have a friend. Then Janelle smiled because she had just found a new friend in the image of herself. Janelle said she used to talk, sing, dance, and do everything with her friend in the mirror.

Though she never bothered to give her friend a name, Janelle's little playmate knew their time together was oooh-so-special. In fact, Janelle thought her friend in the mirror was better than a best friend because they never had arguments and her friend would never talk back.

The thought of having an imaginary friend still makes Janelle laugh, but she especially finds humor in recalling the day her older sister came to visit.

Janelle looked into the mirror at her imaginary friend and said, "Well, I gotta go now. My sister is here, so I don't have to talk to you anymore!"

But that was quite all right with Janelle's friend—she knew it was just a matter of time before Janelle would be standing there telling her all about the visit with her big sister.

From Canada with Love

Sandra, Shirley, and Sharon were but a handful of little black Canadian girls living in Winnipeg in the early 1960s. Each of their families settled in Canada after slavery—it became the homeland of many freed slaves. The happy threesome laughed at all-night sleep-over parties, talked about boys, and went everywhere together. But the tight-knit circle was torn apart when Shirley was shipped off to live with relatives in Antigua when she and her stepfather could not get along.

The girls were devastated and brokenhearted. They wrote letters back and forth and shared secrets long distance. Every Christmas, Shirley returned home and the girls would reminisce about the good times and make plans for their future, promising to always be friends, no matter what. It was an idealistic promise made by three young girls, but it was never broken, even as they blossomed into women. In fact, now they have a lot more in common.

They all have successful careers, live in the United States, and are married to foreigners. When they return home to Winnipeg for the holidays they still giggle and talk about their youth. They also thank each other for keeping their promise to remain lifelong friends.

My Angel, My Friend

It was 34 years ago when Vernelle Hunt became a member of Mt. Olive Baptist Church. There were many churches in Vernelle's new town, but she believed the Lord led her and her four children to Mt. Olive to grow in grace. Shortly after joining the church, Vernelle was befriended by Deaconess Hazel Hunt, a mother of five.

"We seemed to hit it off right from the start," Vernelle told me. "She quickly became my closest friend and confidante.

With nine children between us, we had a lot to talk about. Over the years, we have been there for each other, whether it was to talk, cry, or complain."

Their friendship was anchored in church, and other mothers began to spend time with them, too. In fact, it was Vernelle and Hazel who started the Mt. Olive Mothers' Club. Together, mothers and their children went on day trips and often set up play dates. Through the years, their friendship just seemed to keep on growing. As they became closer to each other, they also became closer to God. And every night when Vernelle said her prayers, she thanked God for sending an angel her way.

Vernelle Hunt died a couple of months ago. At her wake, I handed Hazel a copy of the letter Vernelle sent me about her friendship with Hazel. Hazel hugged me and said "thank you."

Enough Friends

FIVE-YEAR-OLD HOLLY MOVED INTO A NEW NEIGHBORHOOD, leaving her playmates behind. As she sat on the porch of her house, she saw a little girl, about the same size as her, singing aloud and playing with dolls in her backyard.

Holly skipped across the street and peeked through the fence to get a closer look at the pretty little girl with the long, thick ponytails that draped down her back. She was playing with a bunch of black Barbie dolls and even a black Ken doll.

Little Holly squeezed her small frame through an opening in the fence and walked toward the girl.

"Hi. My name is Holly," she said. "What's your name?"

"My name is Jennifer, but my friends call me Jen-Jen," she replied.

The two girls smiled at each other, realizing they were probably the same age.

"Can I be your friend?" Holly asked. "Can I call you Jen-Jen?"

Jennifer stuck her index finger in her mouth as if she had to think it over. She bit on the finger for a few seconds and quickly pulled it out.

"No," Jennifer answered. "I already have enough friends."

Holly looked at Jennifer with a twinge of disappointment and sadness in her eyes. "Pleeeeeease," Holly pleaded.

Jennifer picked up one of her Barbie dolls and brushed

her hair with a teeny-weeny pink comb. Then she looked at Holly and flashed a big bright smile.

"Okay, you can be my friend, but only for today," she said. "And you gotta call me Jen-Jen."

Jen-Jen handed her new pal a doll and an assortment of tiny doll clothing. They giggled and pretended that Barbie and Ken were about to go out on a date.

Holly and Jen-Jen remember that story like it was yesterday, but the truth of the matter is they met 20-something years ago and are still the very best of friends today.

Through Thick and Thin

Dee and Adiya were the only two caramel-colored second graders at a recently integrated elementary school in South Carolina. The year was 1963 and African-Americans were still called colored folks or niggers.

Adiya was bused to the predominantly white school from the other side of the tracks, where she lived in a one-bedroom wooden shack with her mother and two brothers. Her family was so poor that parishioners at a local Baptist church supplied them with clothes, shoes, and toys.

All of her classmates knew by the metal tokens she handed the cafeteria aide that she was the recipient of free lunch—a stigma so embarrassing that nobody else in the class, not even Dee, wanted to be associated with her.

You see, Dee did not have it so bad. Her father was the only black doctor and they lived in a lavish two-story home in the white section of town. Yet not even Daddy's money could gain his precious sweetheart access to the "white-only" public school, a block away from their house, until integration became the law. But even still, Dee fit in right away. She already had a lot of neighborhood friends who had come to like and accept her.

Poor Adiya, on the other hand, had a much harder time. She was the only other black girl in the class, and no one knew her. Instead of making an effort to get to know her, everyone teased her, even Dee. Adiya didn't have a friend in the whole school. And she ate alone every day.

One day, a few older boys sat down beside Adiya and began taunting her. She paid them no mind; she was too busy filling her tummy with her free lunch.

"Slow down," one boy yelled at Adiya. "I know you don't have any food at home, but you could show some manners."

"That's right," another boy chimed in. "You niggers act like animals when you eat."

Dee couldn't believe her ears. By this time, a crowd had gathered at the table. Adiya began to cry, the tears tickling into her mouth as she continued eating. She never spoke a word.

"You hear us talking to you, nigger?" the first boy said. "Stop eating and look at us when we are talking to you."

The moment Adiya looked up, he poured a cup of strawberry gelatin over her head. All the kids in the cafeteria laughed and began throwing food at Adiya. The spectacle became so noisy, a teacher walked over to see what happened. Dee stood frozen, unable to speak.

"Get away from her," the teacher said, shooing the crowd away. She looked at Adiya and laughed. "You sure are one pitiful sight."

Dee felt so bad for Adiya that she cried, too. Her mama and daddy warned her that some people might call her names or treat her badly simply because she was black, but until today she never realized exactly what they meant. Dee rushed to Adiya's side, wiped her tears, and helped gather her belongings.

"Don't worry—it will be okay," Dee told her. "Those kids are mean and stupid."

Adiya looked at Dee and said, "Then why do you like hanging around them?"

"I wanted them to like me," Dee replied. "I'm sorry I didn't play with you. Will you be my friend?"

"Sure," Adiya said, still wiping food off her clothes. "I don't pay nobody at school no mind—nobody but the teacher. Mama told me to study hard so I can grow up to be somebody."

"You already are," Dee said. "I'm sorry if I was mean before, but I am sort of glad it happened because otherwise I wouldn't have talked to you. I think we are going to be good friends."

And they were. From that day on, Dee and Adiya stuck together like glue. And Dee learned an important lesson. The true friends in life are not those who tease and taunt others to make themselves look better. A true friend likes you for who you are and will stand by you through thick and thin.

All Grown Up

$\mathcal{K}$AREN AND ANITA WERE FRIENDS SINCE CHILDHOOD. AFTER they graduated from high school, Karen went to college and Anita went to work as a waitress. They lost touch, as do a lot of high school friends, but thought about each other often.

Years later, their paths unexpectedly crossed. Karen, a computer specialist, was dining at a Manhattan restaurant when she looked up and recognized her waitress. It was Anita.

"Ooh my god," Anita said.

"Anita?" Karen beamed. "Is that you?"

They embraced each other. They were both in their 40s, but life had obviously been rougher on Anita. Crow's-feet had already begun to outline Anita's almond eyes and a frown was etched into her forehead. Yet beneath the surface, Karen could still see her beautiful playmate—the one who used to sleep over and taught her how to stuff her bra with tissue paper. The same Anita who climbed the big maple when Karen's cat was stuck, simply because Karen was too scared of heights to rescue it herself.

"You look wonderful," Anita said, obviously in awe of her childhood friend. "I always knew you would make it. Don't tell me—you are an accountant just like you set out to be."

"Yes and no," Karen said. "I am an accountant, but I am working in the computer business."

The women talked about their escapades all night and exchanged telephone numbers.

Karen made several attempts to reach Anita, but her phone was out of service. Finally, she returned to the restaurant and found Anita waiting tables. But this time Anita was not as friendly. She claimed she was too busy to talk, obviously embarrassed about something.

"I'm going through a tough time," Anita said. "My old man and I split up and he left me with a stack of bills and three growing children."

"Say no more," Karen said. "Call me when you get off and we'll go somewhere to talk. If you can't talk to a friend, who can you turn to?"

Anita reluctantly agreed, and later that night the women talked for hours. Karen offered her money, but Anita didn't want any handouts. Instead she wanted a good secure job where she didn't have to be on her feet all night and could spend more time at home with her children.

As if she sprinkled magic dust, or had a special connection with an angel, Karen called Anita the very next day with good news.

"If you are serious and willing to work hard, I think I have a job for you," Karen beamed. "A business associate of mine is looking for an assistant to answer telephones, set up appointments, and help out around the office. The job is yours if you want it."

"I'd love it," Anita said. "When do I start?"

"On Monday, if you can swing it," Karen said. "And don't bother to thank me—it's the least I could do for an old friend who saved my cat's life several times and never teased me about being afraid of heights."

To Anita's surprise, the salary was more than she ever imagined and her children were covered under her new insurance plan. The job was a dream come true. After just a few weeks Anita was able to pay her rent, buy a used car, and treat her children to a few special outings. Best of all, she was home early enough to tuck her kids in at night.

"How can I possibly thank you?" Anita asked her friend.

"You can thank me by coming back into my life again," Karen replied. "I haven't had a good friend around in years and I forgot how great it is."

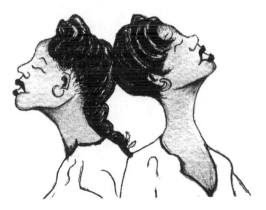

The Ties That Bind

The Golden Gals

LILLIE, CARRIE, AND MABEL ALL MISSED THEIR 10TH, 25TH, and 40th high school reunions, but they vowed to meet in Florida for their 50th reunion. Lillie lived in Detroit, Carrie in Chicago, and Mabel in New York, and though they visited each other regularly over the years, this was the first time the friends traveled without their husbands, children, or grandchildren!

They met at the airport, each glamorous in her own right, decked out in flashy designer clothing, jewelry, and hats cocked to the side. Lillie, Carrie, and Mabel had all married well and it showed. Lillie's husband was a doctor, Carrie's was a high-powered civil rights attorney, and Mabel's owned a popular restaurant. The old friends hugged and made their way to a limousine. As they drove into their hometown, the women chatted nonstop about their lives and how far they'd come since childhood.

When they reached the town, Mabel immediately recognized a familiar face. It was William, Carrie's old boyfriend who still worked construction in the same town.

"There's William," Mabel screeched as the car slowed down.

"Your prom date," Lillie giggled. "I still remember that pink dress and those greasy tight-ass curls."

"Stop the car," Carrie screamed. She and Mabel went to speak to him. William couldn't believe his eyes. He immediately recognized his high school sweetheart who was just as beautiful as she was 50 years ago.

"See you at the reunion," Carrie said after a brief conversation. "Save me a dance, if your wife won't mind," Carrie innocently flirted.

"Sure thing," William said shyly. "See you there."

Lillie refused to get out of the car. To her, William was hardly worth the effort. He had failed to move on in life and in her eyes she and her friends were royalty. She poked fun at Carrie and Mabel for talking to William.

"If you had married William, you wouldn't be the wife of an influential civil rights attorney," Lillie said. "William never could have provided you with a good life."

Carrie looked at Lillie and rolled her eyes.

"Still a snob after all these years," Carrie shot back. "Some things never change."

"That's for sure," Mabel said, coming to Carrie's defense. "Had Carrie married William, then William would have been the civil rights attorney," Mabel said. "We all know that behind every successful man is a good woman. And just between girlfriends, we also know that Carrie got her husband where he is today."

"Okay, Mabel, I have to agree on that," Lillie said, giving her friends a thumbs-up. "Our husbands are lucky to have us in their corner."

Kimberly's Other Mother

Carol's son, Darren, was quite a catch—handsome, smart, charming, successful—a real ladies' man. The problem was he knew it. Carol met so many of Darren's girlfriends that she couldn't keep them straight. Few of them came around more than once or twice before Darren brought a new girl home. Finally, Carol warned Darren not to bring another woman around unless he was serious about her. Months passed by. Carol's son didn't bring any of his dates home, just like his mother asked, and then Kimberly appeared. She was every mother's dream. Beautiful. Loving. Ambitious. And just as smart and worldly as Carol's Harvard-educated son.

At first, Carol tried to keep her distance, figuring she'd be out of the picture soon, but Kimberly's outgoing personality was infectious. The women quickly won each other's heart. Kimberly loved spending time with Carol and began inviting her to tag along to dinner and the movies with her and Darren. Darren was also pleased the two hit it off so well, since his parents had recently divorced. When Darren was out of town on business, Kimberly took Carol shopping and to dinner. They even enjoyed overnight trips to Atlantic City to play the slot machines and split their winnings.

Kimberly had found herself another mother and Carol thought her son had finally settled down. Yet, to their surprise and dismay, Darren broke up with Kimberly six months into the relationship. Both women were heartbroken, but they vowed to remain friends.

"Darren may have introduced us, but he had nothing to do with our friendship," Carol told Kimberly. "I hope we can continue to be friends."

"Me too," Kimberly replied. "I wouldn't have it any other way."

Deep down inside, Carol prayed her son and Kimberly would reunite and give her the grandchild she longed for. Each night she'd pray for God to work things out, but weeks turned into months, and eventually a year passed by. Kimberly and Carol did remain friends, though it was awkward for some time. But eventually, Kimberly met another young man, who she fell in love with and married.

Carol feared she would lose touch with Kimberly, but in fact the opposite happened. Not only was Carol invited to the wedding but she was seated with Kimberly's family. Carol bragged to guests that she was Kimberly's "other mother." And a year later, at Kimberly's baby shower, she joked that she was thrilled to finally become a grandma. Just like a mother, Carol was there when Kimberly gave birth to an 8-pound baby girl, and the little girl was raised believing she had three grandmothers.

Grandma Carol spoiled her "granddaughter" with cards, toys, and savings bonds. On a visit with Kimberly, Carol confessed something she had been carrying around for a long time.

"In my heart, I'm still sad that you're not my daughter-in-law," she said. "But I thank God for blessing me with a special friend. I love you."

We'll Do It Together

MARSHA AND JACKIE WERE COLLEGE ROOMMATES. BOTH WERE from small towns in Kentucky and grew up on farms. But they had much more in common than that. You see, their parents had the same first names, they were born on the same day, their boyfriends played on the same college football team, and they pledged the same sorority. Over their four-year college stay, Marsha and Jackie spent many nights planning and dreaming about having a double wedding ceremony and starting families.

After graduation, the roommates were able to pull off a beautiful double wedding ceremony and managed to find jobs and houses in the same town. The first years of marriage were a lot of fun and the newlyweds spent lots of time together.

Jackie was the first to get pregnant; she gave birth to a beautiful little girl. Marsha and her husband, Thomas, tried to get pregnant, but something was wrong. They tried all kinds of fertility drugs, but nothing seemed to work. Marsha and Thomas became frustrated and the blissful marriage was suddenly on the rocks—each blamed the other for the infertility problem. Eventually, the doctor determined that Marsha was indeed unable to have children, and since she wanted to be a mom more than anything in the world, she became depressed and tried to commit suicide after the terrible news.

Jackie helped Marsha recover. She was very compassionate and loving toward her best friend. As weeks passed, Marsha went back to work and she spent time with friends again. When Jackie thought Marsha was truly ready to come to grips with her inability to have children, she talked to her about adoption.

"Being a mommy isn't just giving birth," Jackie said. "It's sharing love and cultivating a naive and innocent little child into a responsible adult. If you are half as caring with your child as you are with mine, you'll be just fine."

Marsha talked it over with Thomas and he agreed. They found an agency and soon Marsha was feeding, burping, and changing a beautiful baby girl, who they named Jackie, after her mom's best friend. Little Jackie looked so much like her adoptive parents, it was eerie. The new baby healed Marsha and Thomas's marriage, and suddenly their future seemed bright again.

One day, when Marsha was alone with her daughter, she whispered in the infant's ear: "My only hope for you is that you meet a special girlfriend in college who will stick by you through thick and thin, and I also hope you pledge Delta, just like mommy and Auntie Jackie."

Rats in the Front Room

DID YOU EVER HAVE ONE OF THOSE FRIENDS WHO COULD TALK you into anything no matter how stupid? Or perhaps you were the one who was doing the convincing. Well that's how it was for Felecia and Terri, who had been friends since they were 2 years old. They grew up in the same housing complex in Detroit and they did everything together.

Terri was the adventurous one who lived on the edge, and Felecia followed Terri's every lead. When they were 8 years old, Terri convinced Felecia to stand on the ledge of her fourth-floor apartment, promising to follow. As soon as Felecia stepped out the window, her mother walked in and gave her a spanking.

When they were 11 years old, Terri assured Felecia that her mother would buy her a brand new bicycle, if only she ran away from home.

"Your mama will be so glad to see you come home," Terri said. "She'll buy you any bike in the store, maybe even the Deluxe Schwinn with the flowered basket. It worked for me."

Felecia wrote a note, grabbed her favorite book and a blanket, and met Terri outside their fourteen-story building. Felecia jumped on the back of Terri's bike and off they went. Despite their efforts, the girls only made it fifteen blocks before they were spotted by a family friend. Once again, Felecia got a spanking. And the bike? Forget about it. Terri's plan backfired.

But the one story that remains etched in both their minds is the one they refer to as "Rats in the Front Room."

It was a freezing day in the Motor City. Terri's mother sent her to the drugstore to pay the telephone bill. Terri didn't want to go alone, so she stopped by Felecia's house and persuaded her to come along.

Felecia wrapped herself in her warmest coat—a tan full-length sheepskin coat that she was only allowed to wear to church. Felecia had no business wearing the coat, but as usual Terri convinced her she'd be fine.

"Just wear it," she insisted. "No one will know." And of course, Felecia listened. What Felecia didn't know was that Terri had planned to make a pit stop at a classmate's house who lived in the worst housing project in Detroit. The two 18-year-olds walked in the dilapidated building, stepping over piles of trash and holding their nose as the smell of urine filled the air. They walked up three flights of stairs, occasionally tripping over steps that had started to crumble. The girls were scared. As they made their way to their classmate's door, they started singing the popular Grand Master Flash & the Furious Five rap song called "The Message": *Rats in the front room . . . junkies in the alley with a baseball bat.*

Before they knocked on their friend's door, a man wearing a black mask jumped out from nowhere.

"Give me your coat," he screamed at Felecia, brandishing a huge switchblade. Both girls screamed. And to Felecia's surprise, Terri jumped in front of her.

"All right, all right, don't hurt us. We'll give you what you want, but you *can't* have her coat," Terri said as calmly as possible.

Instead, Terri reached into her pocket and pulled out the $150 that her mother gave her to pay the telephone bill.

"Here, take this," Terri said as she threw the crisp bills at his feet. "It's a hundred and fifty bucks—now leave us alone."

The masked man quickly gathered the money that flew in circles around his feet and the girls fled outside into the courtyard. When they stopped to catch their breath, Felecia exclaimed, "Oh my God, Terri—you saved our lives!" She hugged her friend and asked, "What about your mama's money—she's going to kill you."

"I know," said Terry. "But it won't be with a hunting knife. She'll torture me to death. I can live with that. Besides, you've been taking the rap for all of our escapades for the last 18 years. It's about time I took the blame. I'm just glad we're alive. So anyway, let's get you home and out of that coat before your mom catches you wearing it, and then we'll go deal with my mother."

"Thanks Terri," Felecia said. "You may have gotten us into this mess, but you also got us out of it. I appreciate it."

"No problem," Terri replied, and the two walked side by side down the street like they had done so many times before. Without having to say a word, both knew their friendship had taken a turn for the better.

Friends 'Til the End

It was a warm and sunny Florida day when Gladys walked into little 3-year-old Sarah Jean's life. Gladys, a tall, thin, middle-aged black woman, strolled into the yard. The blue-eyed, blond-haired toddler was a bit leery of the stranger.

Gladys kneeled down and stared into the girl's face. Sarah Jean smiled and ran into the house. Gladys followed.

"You must be Gladys," Sarah Jean's mother said in a Southern drawl. "Come right in and let me get you a cold drink. Grab a seat."

Sarah Jean's mother was pregnant with twins and needed help around the house. Gladys was hired to be the nanny and immediately became a part of Sara Jean's family.

Gladys spent her days at Sarah Jean's house—cooking, cleaning, and making sure everything was in place—and every night Gladys went home to her husband and four children.

The fact that Gladys was black and Sarah Jean's family was white was irrelevant. They were extended family members. The families felt lucky to have each other and treated each other with kindness, love, and respect through the years.

Before long, Sarah Jean was off to elementary school, softball practices, ballet, piano lessons, and summer camp. In a blink of an eye, Sarah Jean had bloomed into a beautiful young woman. Gladys watched adoringly as she celebrated her sweet sixteen, dated, and then graduated from high school and college.

With each different phase in Sarah Jean's life, Gladys was always there listening to her problems, advising her about her love life, and promising never to reveal Sarah Jean's secrets. No matter what!

Sarah Jean and Gladys had become friends. Gladys was there when Sarah Jean got married, had her first child, and bought her first house in Boston. They always remained in close touch.

So when Sarah Jean got word that Gladys had a stroke, she hopped on a plane and rushed to Gladys's bedside to hold her friend's hand and comfort her.

Gladys and Sarah Jean laughed about the old times. Like the time Sara Jean got caught sneaking out her bedroom window to go to a party and claimed that she was about to wash the windows so that Gladys wouldn't have to. When Gladys found out, she really did make Sarah Jean wash them. And the day Gladys showed up at Sarah Jean's science fair bragging that her project was the best and told the teacher it would behoove her to give Sarah Jean an A. It was hard to believe how fast time went by, but they laughed and cried at the many memories they shared.

Sarah Jean went back home to Boston and four days later Gladys passed on. Sarah Jean wept for a day. She had lost her nanny, her surrogate mother—and in a sense her best friend.

Sarah Jean returned to Florida for Gladys's funeral and

was touched to find that the funeral program listed Sarah Jean, the twins, and her parents as "extended family members." Gladys's family also asked Sarah Jean to say a few words, knowing how much it would mean to Gladys. Sarah Jean eagerly agreed.

"For me, there are hardly any memories of growing up that didn't involve Gladys," Sarah Jean said in front of all the friends and family who came to pay their respects. "She taught me more than how to cook collard greens; she taught me that family doesn't have to be your own flesh and blood. Even though Gladys would never admit I was the most difficult child—and I know I was—she taught me how to love."

Sarah Jean stepped away from the podium and walked over to the mahogany casket. She softly kissed Gladys and whispered, "Good-bye, my friend. Your spirit lives on in me."

You Know She's a
True Friend Because . . .

- She'll let the UPS man drop off your QVC purchases at her house to prevent your man from pitching a fit.

- She will say your outfit is too tight, too ugly, or too much when you thought it was stunning.

- She will discreetly slip you a mint when you're having a bad breath day.

- She will approach a handsome stranger on your behalf and introduce you.

- She will babysit, house-sit, or animal-sit on late notice.

- She knows your fears and insecurities and helps you avoid them at all cost.

- She would never, ever sleep with your man or your ex (for that matter) even if he had the body of an NFL linebacker or were as fine as Denzel.

- She would never read your diary, even if it were open and on the table.

- She attends your child's annual spring concert every year, though your son can't sing.

- She ate your mom's meatloaf and asked for the recipe, though everyone else trashed it.

- She lets you take your frustrations out on her and then she forgives you.

- She is willing to make prank calls to your boss after he gives you a hard time.

- She will make you laugh when you really want to cry.

- She promises that you will also be a millionaire when she hits the lottery.

- She will not judge you for wanting to have one last fling even though she is going to be the maid of honor at your June wedding.

- She will whip up a tasty meal for you and your date because you told him you could cook.

- She will remind you that you are still beautiful, even though you gained 50 pounds during your pregnancy and can't seem to trim down.

- She will anonymously send you flowers when you are at the end of your rope.

- She forgives you for returning a Christmas gift she bought you.

- She cosigns your lies and swears it's the truth, though there are holes in your story.

- She will get out of bed at 3 A.M. and drive you two towns over to what's-her-name's house to reassure you that your man's car is not parked outside—if it is, she will help you trash it.

- She'd never pull out a calculator to itemize a restaurant check.

- She will help you cheat on your diet, then make sure you run an extra lap.

- She will never embarrass you in public or in front of your colleagues.

- She would only tell your secrets if your life depended on it.

Too Blessed to Be Stressed

THE MINUTE TONYA AND KARA WALKED INTO A SEMINAR FOR executives of their company, the two African-American women bonded. They waited for another black man or black woman to walk into the meeting, but to no avail. Besides the hotel workers, they were the only ones in the room who had dark skin.

Few words were spoken, but their connection was automatic. They struggled to remain focused, but at each break they were baffled that a large company would only have two senior black employees. At the end of the day when they finally got a chance to talk in depth, Tonya and Kara expressed concern about their positions and how each of them were questioned and second-guessed by those who worked under them.

"I do a lot of praying," Kara said. "I ask the Lord to give me strength to make it through each day."

"Me too!" Tonya said. "I've even tried to talk to my boss about it and he basically told me that I shouldn't look at everything in black and white or male and female."

The more they talked, the more their stories, situations, and careers seemed to mirror each other. Kara worked in Jacksonville and Tonya worked in Manhattan, but racism, bigotry, and prejudice thrived in both of their offices. They would get complaints from other black staffers that their coworkers were constantly telling racial jokes, making off-the-cuff remarks about notable African-Americans, or circulating insulting e-mail messages.

Their white employees said Kara and Tonya favored the black workers, and blacks said they favored the whites. It was uncomfortable for the women, but they felt relief in knowing there was at least one other person out there who truly understood their dilemma. So before the women left the seminar, they made a pact to speak to each other every morning and every night in order to provide some sort of support and encouragement.

Like clockwork, Kara, the self-proclaimed early riser, gave Tonya a wake-up call. They would pray for patience and endurance, then follow up by singing a few verses of a soul-stirring gospel song. And when that wasn't enough, they would call each other during the day to get advice and inspiration. Then, just before Tonya went to sleep, she would call Kara to make sure her day went smoothly. Again, they'd pray and give thanks for getting through another day. Tonya would end each conversation by saying, "We are too blessed to be stressed!"

A Yam, I Am

$\mathcal{L}$ILLIAN, LESLIE, CAROLYN, SHARON, AND CHARNETTE ARE Yams. That's right, yams! They call themselves Sisters of the Yam, a name adapted from one of bell hooks's books, *Sisters of the Yam*.

You see, the Yams are all choir members at Bethany Baptist Church in Newark, New Jersey. The women wanted to get together outside of the church setting, so Leslie decided to invite everyone to her house back in 1990. The five friends had so much fun they pledged to get together at least four times a year. The women thought it would be fun to celebrate their birthdays together.

And their birthday gatherings are not just ice cream and cake; they are adventures created around a theme of the hostess's choice. While some like to pull out the fine china to entertain the Yams, one party was at Martha's Vineyard.

"Our parties are truly beautiful," Lillian told me. "We are sure to make each Yam feel extra special on her birthday. There is a lot of love between us."

The Yams have been to see Kirk Franklin in concert, a ballet, and even line dancing. Sure, they were the only sistahs at the Country and Western Club, but it didn't give them the honkey-tonk blues. They had lots of fun. The entertainment is just one aspect of the birthday celebration. There's lots of good food, great company, and who could overlook the beautifully wrapped gifts. Gifts have included a piece of original art, a mountain bike, and even a necklace from Tiffany's. The friends chip in to get each Yam something from her birthday wish list, and individuals buy gifts, too. Then the hostess usually surprises each Yam with a favor-like gift, which at one party was a 30-minute massage.

"We are sisters and friends," Lillian said. "We support each other and truly enjoy our network. The Yams are always there to make our lives more pleasant."

Just when the Yams thought they had run out of new and original ideas, one girlfriend had five 14-karat gold rings with stones made for each Yam. And after the rings were made, the mold was destroyed. The friendship these five friends share is so special and unique that they've decided to keep it just between them.

"We just have a good time together," Lillian said. "Other women want to get in, but it's closed. We've really bonded."

These Yams say they want to keep their fancy birthday parties private, but encourage other women to socialize and pamper each other more often. There's something really sweet about these potatoes—they've found strength in the Yams.

Heard It Through the Grapevine

SADIE AND SHIRLEY'S FRIENDSHIP SPANNED THREE DECADES. The women were introduced by their husbands, Donald and Teddy, when they were newlyweds, and from that day on they became best friends.

They raised their children down the street from each other, went on vacations together, and spent hours upon hours on the telephone every week, despite the fact that they were neighbors. To their surprise and delight, Sadie and Shirley became first-time grandmothers on the very same day. But what was not so nice was how it affected their friendship.

Sadie's daughter lived on the West Coast, so she didn't get a chance to see her grandson very often. But Shirley's granddaughter, Maya, lived less than an hour away and she got to see her all the time.

When Shirley was given the choice of babysitting for Maya or going to her favorite jazz club with her friends, she would always pick babysitting. Shirley documented Maya's every achievement—the first time she smiled, sat up, slept all night, crawled, talked, and walked. You name it, Shirley captured it all on video camera and spent countless hours putting together scrapbooks and time capsules. Though at first everyone figured Shirley was just a proud first-time grandma, her behavior bordered on obsessive.

Donald, Shirley's husband, complained to Teddy about Shirley's behavior, knowing he would tell Sadie, who would immediately tell Shirley. He was right.

"I know you love Maya," Sadie said. "We all do, but Donald is feeling a bit neglected. You're never around anymore."

"That's ridiculous," Shirley snapped, cutting her off. "I'm her grandmother. She needs me."

"I am just trying to help," Sadie said. "I don't want you to hurt Donald or get hurt yourself."

What Sadie really wanted to tell her was that she was hurt, too. She missed her friend, but she didn't have the nerve to tell her.

Shirley ignored Sadie's advice and continued to spend more time with her granddaughter than her husband. Eventually, Shirley stopped going out altogether. The quartet became a threesome, Donald always being the odd man out. Before long they simply stopped asking Shirley to go out with them, hoping she would notice, but Shirley was too wrapped up in Maya to notice or care.

The situation got worse. A healthy and loving marriage had quickly turned old and cold. If Shirley wasn't at her son's house, Maya was at Granny's house. Donald was at the end of his rope, and Shirley was so selfish she didn't even notice, but Sadie did. And Sadie was not about to let her friend lose her husband and everything she cared about in life. Since Shirley wouldn't listen, Sadie devised a plan.

At the nail salon one day, the manicurist asked Shirley, "So is it true that you and Donald are splitting up?"

"Splitting up? Hell no," Shirley said, turning three shades of red. "Where did you hear that?"

"Through the gossip grapevine," she said. "No one sees you together anymore, and let's face it, people are talking. You know there are a bunch of women in town who would love to sweep Donald away. He's a good man, Shirley. Be careful."

Shirley left the salon in a huff, embarrassed and feeling guilty. She stopped by Donald's job, offering to treat him to lunch, but he claimed he had a meeting. Her next stop was Sadie's, but she wasn't home. Finally, Shirley went home and called Teddy, but he didn't take her call.

Shaken, Shirley began to recount the last few months. Since the birth of Maya, she *had* ignored Donald. And Sadie and Teddy, too. But she would never want to lose Donald, or her best friend. She knew she had to act fast. She prayed that Donald and her friends would forgive her.

That night, she invited Sadie and Teddy over for dinner and prepared Donald's favorite meal—roasted lamb chops with a raspberry mint sauce, scallop potatoes, and fresh string beans. The foursome laughed and talked like old times. Shirley marveled at how lucky she was to have a husband and friends who were willing to forgive and forget.

Shirley even pulled out her wedding album with pictures from their Las Vegas honeymoon. Donald was all smiles, thinking about all the hopes and dreams they had, and Sadie and Shirley laughed like schoolgirls over the funny memories they shared.

"I'm very sorry," Shirley said. "I hope you will forgive me."

"We made a vow to grow old together, baby," Donald said. "And here we are, just like we planned. Like a bottle of fine wine, our relationship just seems to get better with time."

Shirley held up her glass and proposed a toast.

"Here's to more wonderful memories. For all of us!"

Shirley and Donald sealed their words with a kiss. Sadie and Teddy finished their drinks and quietly left the two lovebirds alone. Shirley knew her marriage was back on track, but she didn't realize she really owed it all to her friend Sadie.

The next day, Shirley's manicurist called Sadie.

"So did it work?" she asked. "Did Shirley believe that people were really gossiping about her marriage?"

"Yesss, of course," Sadie said. "You must have been very convincing. Thanks for playing along, and don't ever mention this conversation to Shirley."

Sadie hung up the telephone and smiled. It was a bit underhanded, but when it came down to the possibility of trouble in paradise Sadie was willing to go to the wire for her friend. And she would do it again if need be, but Sadie was pretty convinced that this was exactly the scare her friend needed to get her back on track. At times she was tempted to tell her friend that she was responsible for saving her marriage, but in retrospect she knew it was not necessary. Between girlfriends, some things are better left unsaid.

Have a Little Faith

I WAS IN GREENVILLE, SOUTH CAROLINA, AT A BOOKSTORE when two young women walked through the door and headed to the back of the store where I sat signing copies of my first book, *Mama Knows Best*.

Kayla was pregnant, and her friend April insisted that Kayla sit next to me while she stood at the end of the line. Once their books were signed, the three of us started chatting. I told them that I was writing a second book about girl-friends and had already begun collecting stories.

"Is the same artist doing the cover?" Kayla asked.

"No. In fact, I am looking for another African-American woman to do the art for the next book," I replied. Just then Kayla's eyes popped out of her head.

"Well, April is an extraordinary artist," Kayla raved. "Seriously, you've got to see her work. She's amazing. She would do an excellent job for you."

April blushed, never saying a word as her friend continued to sing her praises. Finally, Kayla asked which hotel I was staying in and what time April could bring her work over. April, embarrassed, finally spoke up.

"Kayla, give her a break," April mused. "I'm sure she's got better things to do."

"I'm just doing what any friend would do, especially knowing your talent, girl," Kayla answered. "Give *yourself* a break. Show her your stuff."

And she did. Two hours later, April was in my hotel room sheepishly showing me greeting cards, prints, bookmarks, and cloth bags that donned her artwork. I immediately realized her girlfriend was not just talking her up—this lady truly was amazing.

One thing led to another, and I spent the next couple of weeks negotiating and planning for April to draw some of the illustrations inside this book.

"I owe it all to Kayla," April said. "There's nothing like having a girlfriend who believes in you and is willing to go out of her way to let everyone know it. I will always be grateful to her for this opportunity. I only hope I can somehow return the favor because that's what friends are for."

Girlfriend to Girlfriend

We can't pick our family, but thank God we can pick our own friends. I must say, I've picked some good ones.

Rose
Hartford, CT

Friends give us the confidence we need. They push us to strive harder and believe in us even when we don't believe in ourselves.

Annie
Manhattan, NY

When it comes to friendship, quality is much more important than quantity. I would rather have a few friends who truly love me than dozens who don't remember my birthday.

Carol
Atlanta, GA

A good friendship is a lot like a fine wine—it gets better with age and time.

Edith
Brooklyn, NY

If you cannot agree to sometimes disagree, you cannot be friends.

Josephine
Houston, TX

When all else fails, I call my best friend. She has a way of wiping my tears and calming my fears.

Leslie
Charlotte, NC

Before there were therapists, there were girlfriends.

Mary
Chicago, IL

Friends who pray together, stay together.

Shavon
Washington, DC

The silence of a true friend speaks louder than the best advice of an acquaintance

Betty
Providence, RI

In order to *have* a good friend, you must *be* a good friend. Oftentimes women demand more of their friends than they are willing to give of themselves.

Michelle
Manhattan, NY

When it all boils down, I would rather have one *faithful* friend than a whole bunch of mediocre ones.

Debra
Phoenix, AZ

Men come and go, but best friends are forever.

Belinda
Norfolk, VA

Friendship is truly a gift from God. Cherish all the good times, overlook some of the bad times, and pray for laughter.

Christine
Tampa, FL

Thick as Thieves

ANNIE AND BENILDA WERE BEST FRIENDS AND AS THICK AS thieves. Benilda was there when Annie married Floyd, a high-profile celebrity. Though everyone was thrilled about the wedding—even Benilda—things quickly turned sour. The celebrity status came with an ego and Floyd thought he could get away with doing whatever he wanted to Annie, including dishing out a few black eyes and bruises. When they had children, he ruled their 10-bedroom mansion with an iron fist, and even their two sons feared him.

But when it came time to smile pretty for the cameras, Floyd always flashed a grin. He played the part and Annie hid her bruises. Benilda desperately tried to convince Annie to get help, but her self-esteem was too low. Instead, she justified Floyd's abuse by saying she had deserved it. This infuriated Benilda, but every time she brought the subject up, Annie got mad.

Benilda feared if she kept hounding Annie she would lose her friendship. So instead she tried to be there for her friend and to add some fun to her horrid life.

No matter how much pain Annie was in, Benilda's words were always soothing. Benilda constantly made silly threats about what she was going to do to Floyd. Like the day she wanted to lock him in the closet, or the time she offered to pay to have him roughed up. But on a more serious note Benilda also cautioned Annie about keeping abreast of the family's assets.

"You need to know more about Floyd's finances," Benilda cautioned. "Don't get so caught up living in this mansion that you forget what it was like to be poor."

Finally, after seven years of marriage, a few sexually transmitted diseases, broken ribs, and child support payments to a half dozen illegitimate children, Annie had enough. She packed her bags, and she and the boys moved closer to her family in Alabama.

Meanwhile, Floyd wasted no time replacing Annie. Within a week, he had a young beautiful girl by his side. He took her to all the fine restaurants, but Floyd refused to send money to his wife and kids.

Annie was barely surviving, but she couldn't bring herself to take him to court. She wanted to prove she could make it on her own and landed a public relations job to make ends meet.

After a few months, Benilda missed her girlfriend terribly and sent Annie a plane ticket to visit. They went to all their old hangouts and partied into the wee hours of the morning, drinking champagne and reminiscing about the good times. In the short time Annie had been away from Floyd, she had changed—for the better.

She was not the same timid person. She had matured and her confidence grew. It was during that trip that Annie decided to file for a divorce and Benilda happily helped her.

"You wouldn't let me hit him, but now we are going to hit him in his pockets," Benilda said. "You are going to be one rich lady when we get finished with Mr. Floyd."

Finally, Annie agreed to go to court, but after months of

preliminary hearings Floyd was required to pa
mal amounts of money because he squandere..
money. The divorce became so ugly that it was the talk of the
town. To spite Annie, Floyd would show up to each hearing
with his PYT (pretty young thang) on his arm.

The day before the divorce was to be finalized, Floyd's attorney called to say that Floyd had been delayed on a business trip and would not be available for two days. Annie
knew his chick was with him because the media kept close
tabs on his every move.

"Floyd and that little bitch are out of town," Annie said.
"So if he wants to play, then he will have to pay. I still have my
house keys. Let's go over there and see what we can find. I
know he's hiding his money, and since it's not in the bank, I
bet it's in the house."

"Are you serious?" Benilda asked, hesitating for half a
second. "Okay, let's go!"

There was a back way to get to the house that only family
members and close friends knew about. Annie and Benilda
used the keys and went in through the front door. The friends
walked through the house, snooping and digging up everything they could. Soon they found enough paperwork to
prove that Floyd had indeed hid some of his money to avoid
paying Annie, and of all places, he set up an account in his
new girlfriend's name. But Annie knew there had to be some
cash in the house.

"Now where would Floyd and his little bitch hide his
money?" Annie asked.

"Someplace silly I am sure," Benilda joked. "Do you see a toy box?"

They laughed until they cried. Were they crazy to break into the house? Yes, but Benilda reminded Annie that the house was still legally hers and they could not be charged with breaking and entering.

After an hour of searching, they discovered a plastic garbage bag full of money in the linen closet—tens, twenties, fifties, and hundreds—all neatly wrapped and tied with rubber bands. There had to be at least $300,000. Annie cried when she saw the money; she couldn't believe Floyd would hide money from his own children. How could he? She wondered, knowing that he had showered his new girlfriend with diamonds, designer clothing, and lavish vacations.

"Take it all," Benilda said. "The whole damn bag. That would teach that low-down bastard a thing or two."

"No, we can't," Annie answered.

"He'd *never* know we did it," Benilda pleaded. "Let him and his girlfriend fight over the matter. I am sure *she* has access to this plastic bag . . . and remember the tight budget he kept you on? Hel-lo girlfriend! Take the money."

Annie hesistanly reached into the bag and pulled out bundles of money. Tears poured from her eyes. She couldn't take it all, but she had to take some for her children's sake.

"It's not about you, Annie," Benilda reminded her. "Do it for your sons. And if you won't, I sure as hell will."

"Ahh what the hell," Annie screamed as she unraveled the bundles of money and tossed it in the air. The friends laid down in the money and rolled around, just like in the movies. Then Benilda pulled out a Polaroid camera and snapped shots of the money and all the documents that proved he was hiding assets.

"We'll use these pictures in court if we have to," Benilda said. "Stand out of the way so I can show the picture was taken in the house. You can say that someone mailed these pictures to you. God will forgive us."

Annie and Benilda stuffed packs of money into their clothes and scooped up some loose bills from the bottom of the bag. It was like hitting the lottery. The extra money meant that her children didn't have to live on a shoestring anymore. Back home, Benilda popped open a bottle of bubbly and they laughed hysterically at the Polaroid pictures.

"Thank you, Benilda," Annie said, raising her glass to her best friend. "You have always been there for me, always. I really want to thank you."

"That's what friendship is all about, Annie," Benilda said. "I love you and the kids. It broke my heart to watch Floyd rob you of yourself. We are best friends. Of course I wanted to help. Plus, that was fun."

At the final divorce hearing, the judge ruled in Annie's favor and she didn't even have to reveal the pictures. He awarded Annie with the Miami mansion, the Range Rover and the Mercedes, $12,000 a month in alimony and child support, property in the Bahamas, a boat, and the Manhattan condo and its contents, which by the way included several original pieces of art. The judge also ruled that Annie would be entitled to portions of Floyd's future earnings based on the time frame in which certain contracts were signed. Annie considered returning the money she took, then remembered all the nasty things he did. Instead, she donated a portion of it to Floyd's favorite charity and put the rest of the money in bonds to be used for her children's education, just in case their father did not make provisions, as the judge ordered.

Annie sold the house and bought a smaller one, just as beautiful, in Miami—not far from Benilda. She didn't need 10 bedrooms, three garages, or a movie theater in the house. She now had the freedom and the cash to take in a movie at her leisure. And every now and then, when they need a good laugh, Benilda whips out the infamous pictures of them rolling around in Floyd's money. It is their secret—one they hadn't shared with anyone, until now.

Bonding All the Time

WE ALL KNOW THE OLD CLICHE, "MEN COME AND GO, BUT true friends are forever," but this story really brought it home for me.

Vicky had only been dating Michael for four months. She was unsure if their relationship had a future, but she was sure that her period was late. The 27-year-old schoolteacher put off visiting her doctor for as long as she possibly could, but when she could no longer put off the inevitable he confirmed her fear. She was seven weeks pregnant.

Her first thought was *How am I going to tell Mike?* She worried and went over the scenario a million times in her mind. *We've only been dating four months. He'll think I am trying to trap him. Maybe even ask if it's his. How will he act? What will he expect?* She worried.

Vicky thought about explaining it in a letter, leaving a message on his answering machine, or keeping it to herself until she made a decision. But none of Vicky's choices seemed right. The *only* thing she could think of was to call her girlfriends. They'll understand, she reasoned. They'll know what to do, she hoped. When all else fails, lean on your girlfriends. She convinced herself. And so she called them up and invited them to her house that night. Before they could barely sit down, she blurted out the news.

"I am pregnant."

After a moment of stunned silence, the girls broke out in smiles.

"Congratulations," beamed Emily, an older woman and co-worker.

"Way to go," Paula chimed in. And then inevitably . . .

"What did Mike say?"

Bingo! That was the question she was waiting for.

"Well, he doesn't know yet," she confessed. "That's why I need you guys.

"Don't worry," Vicky reassured her friends. "I will tell him. I just wanted to tell you guys first. I don't know what he'll do, but I *know* you guys will support me. The way I see it, he can stick it out with me, end our relationship, or ask me to have an abortion. And I'll take whatever he says into consideration, but the ultimate decision is mine."

A week later, the friends gathered again. To their delight Vicky announced her decision to go through with the pregnancy, even though Mike was not pleased.

"I'm doing it for myself," Vicky said. "Having a child out of wedlock was never in my plans and neither was an abortion. It won't be easy, but I am going to be a mama."

Though Vicky feared her friends might think she was nuts, in fact they were thrilled and even secretly envious. Paula and Theresa longed to be mothers themselves, but neither had a boyfriend or a husband. And Emily was almost 60 and single, and everyone just assumed she never wanted a child.

"I am so proud of you Vicky," Emily said. "You are making the right decision."

"You think?" Vicky asked, surprised. "But you never had kids."

"Actually, I had a son about 35 years ago," Emily said. "He was born with a hole in his heart and he didn't make it. My husband blamed me and a year later we divorced. I was also pregnant one other time, but I didn't go through with it because I wasn't married. Back then it was shameful to have a baby out of wedlock."

"Do you have any regrets?" Vicky asked.

"Of course I do," Emily said. "I'm close to 60 years old, tenured, and financially secure, but I have no one to share my life with. It's obviously too late for me to have a baby now, but oh how I wished I had that child years ago when I was single. That's why I am so happy for you."

They hugged and then it was silent.

"Have your baby and don't look back," Emily said. "I'm proud of you. You're gonna be a wonderful mother."

"And you'll make an excellent godmother," Vicky blurted out. "If that's okay with you."

"Of course I will," Emily answered. "I would be honored."

"I may not have Mike's support, but thanks to friends like you by my side," Vicky said rubbing her stomach, "this sweet little baby and I will be just fine."

Don't Worry,
Your Secret Is Safe with Me!

WHEN IT COMES TO FRIENDSHIP, KEEPING SECRETS IS VITAL. Whether we want to know their secrets or not, our girlfriends often call on us to listen as they tell us about their most intimate date, greatest pain, personal hardship, or happiest moment. Though they sometimes want our opinion, for the most part they just need to share their deepest feelings with someone who they know will keep their secret close to their heart.

When we were kids, our girlfriends would preface each secret with the phrase "cross your heart and hope to die," and when that wasn't enough they'd add "stick a needle in your eye." And we did each hand gesture to simply prove we were worthy of protecting the secret.

So when I asked African-American women from across the country what secrets they had been entrusted with, it didn't surprise me that anonymity was essential. Here's some of the secrets I've collected. My girlfriend would kill me if she knew I told anyone that she:

- Had sex on a park bench in the middle of the day.
- Switched the tag on a designer dress and bought it at half price.
- Memorized her boyfriend's answering machine code and retrieved his messages.
- Has a crush on her brother-in-law and flirts with him all the time.

- Would have a full mustache if she didn't get electrolysis.
- Is being kept by a wealthy businessman who lives out of town.
- Had a sexual encounter with a woman and enjoyed it.
- Went skinny dipping in a hotel pool in the Bahamas with her man.
- Dyes her hair black because she's completely gray.
- Has a child by a married celebrity and his wife doesn't have a clue.
- Worked for an escort service in college.
- Reads her teenage daughter's diary regularly.
- Went out on a date with an NBA star, drank too much Hennessy, and stood outside the club puking.
- Was raped by her father.
- Produced the drug-free urine that her friend needed for a job.
- Left a Manhattan nightclub with smelly armpits, walked next door to a store, faked like she was going to buy deodorant, sprayed her pits, walked out of the door, and returned to the club.
- Really can't stand her mother-in-law but puts up a good front.
- Aborted a pregnancy when she knew her husband wanted a child.
- Brought a group of guys back to the Atlantic City hotel room where she was vacationing with four girlfriends. They had a party in the room and the guys (all cops) spent the night.

- Has short hair but has worn a weave for years.
- Slept with her boss to get a promotion.
- Dated her husband while he was married to someone else.
- Met her man on the Internet.
- Wears two tampons and a pad when she has her period.
- Had a breast reduction operation.

Just Be Yourself

THEY SAY OPPOSITES ATTRACT. WELL THAT'S HOW IT WAS FOR Amber and Cheryl, two best friends, who were indeed opposites. Amber was a tall, beautiful woman, with an hourglass figure. But even though Amber had the looks to stop men in their tracks, she didn't have the smarts or brains to always hold their attention.

Cheryl, on the other hand, was short, plump, and rather ordinary looking. But what she lacked in looks, she made up for in brains and she enjoyed a successful career as an attorney. Still, she wished men would give her even half the attention they gave to Amber.

After a particularly lonely dry spell, Cheryl placed an ad in the personals. She never told Amber, but she secretly enjoyed receiving letters and phone calls. There was just one little problem. Cheryl didn't have the nerve to tell the men what she *really* looked like, so instead she told them she was tall, thin, and beautiful, like her friend Amber.

Dozens of men wanted to meet this tall and beautiful girl, but Cheryl was just having fun. No dates, just phone calls. The more men called, the more she exaggerated about her looks. The only truth she revealed was about being an attorney.

"Good-looking and smart?" one guy said. "It ought to be illegal."

Cheryl continued to avoid contact by saying she spent a great deal of time working. But one guy, Ernest, refused to give up. He was determined to meet her. They could speak for hours on the phone and they seemed to have everything in common. Finally, Cheryl couldn't resist and she agreed to a date. But as soon as she agreed she realized she'd made a big mistake. He was expecting someone who looked like Amber. He would no doubt be disappointed. She tried to cancel but couldn't get through. Finally, out of desperation, she told Amber what she had done and begged Amber to go in her place.

Amber agreed reluctantly after trying to convince Cheryl she should go. Instead, Cheryl took a seat at a nearby table and watched miserably, while Amber and Ernest enjoyed their date. When the evening was over, Cheryl was upset and accused Amber of coming on to Ernest.

"Well of course I did," Amber cooed. "He's fine. My kind of man. A dentist. Single and looking for a wife."

"But it was *me* he liked on the telephone," Cheryl argued. "Ernest doesn't know anything about you, except what he saw tonight. You don't like museums, the opera, or summers in Martha's Vineyard like we both do."

"But *you're* the one who set me up with him," Amber argued.

For the first time in their lives, Amber and Cheryl were at odds. Both agreed they were wrong for what they did, but neither wanted to give up their chance to be with Ernest. They both went home mad.

Finally, Cheryl realized she had put everyone, especially herself, in an awkward position. Cheryl immediately called

Amber and left a message on her machine: "I know you are mad at me," Cheryl said. "But I am asking you to understand. I asked my best friend to do me a favor. You know more than anyone else that I have a low self-esteem, so I thought you would understand. The truth is that I like Ernest and I want to date him. Will you help me find a way to come clean and tell the truth?"

Amber picked up the phone. "Oh Cheryl, I'm so glad you called. Of course I'll help. I've been thinking about this non-stop. Even though I think Ernest is fine, you guys are meant to be."

The friends laughed and made a vow never to put the other in the middle of a lie again. The next day, Cheryl called Ernest and asked if he could meet her for dinner the following night. "I have something very serious to tell you," Cheryl said. "I pray that you will be able to forgive me."

Ernest agreed to meet her at a cafe that night, and Cheryl spent the rest of the night getting tips from Amber on how to be flirtatious and fun on a date.

"Just be yourself," Amber advised Cheryl. "If Ernest doesn't like you, his loss."

Cheryl called in sick to get ready for her date. Amber was there to hold her hand and reassure her friend that she would be okay, no matter what. Cheryl looked beautiful. She couldn't believe her own eyes. She had been so used to putting herself down that she didn't know how to pick herself up. She drove to the restaurant, took a deep breath, and walked in.

Cheryl recognized Ernest right away. She walked over to the table and sat down.

"Sorry, but that seat is taken," Ernest said. "I'm waiting for someone."

"I think you are waiting for me," she answered.

Ernest blushed. It was obvious that he was intrigued by this mysterious woman. He offered to buy her a drink and reminded her that his date was on her way.

"I am your date, Ernest."

"How did you know my name?"

"I am Cheryl."

"I thought you sounded like her, but you aren't the same Cheryl I met a few days ago."

"Well, I told you that there was something important we needed to talk about," she said. "The beautiful, tall woman you met was my best friend, Amber. It sounds silly, but I was doing a little experiment of my own to see if men wanted beauty or brains."

"I want both," Ernest said. "And if you are who you say you are, why did you sell yourself short? You are beauty and brains."

Cheryl smiled and asked Ernest if he would ever forgive her.

"Before I say yes, is there anything else I need to know?" he asked. "Matter of fact, show me your driver's license, a second picture ID, and a major credit card."

They both laughed. Their date was perfect. Cheryl and Ernest talked until the waiter politely told them the cafe was closing. From the restaurant, they walked through the streets holding hands. As soon as Cheryl got home, she called Amber, who was waiting by the phone for a report.

"Thanks for helping me," Cheryl said. "Only a true friend would have done what you did. And things really went well with Ernest after I confessed."

"You know I've been thinking, and you're right," Amber said. "There was no way I could have kept up the facade. He is fine, but too deep for me. I didn't know who or what he was talking about over dinner, I just enjoyed looking at him. You two are perfect for each other."

The friends laughed, and before they hung up Amber teased, "Now that you found yourself a man, how 'bout handing over those personals. It's my turn now!"

"You got it girlfriend," Cheryl giggled. "Just keep me out of it."

Cheryl hung up the phone and for the first time in a long time she felt beautiful and happy—thanks to Ernest and her best friend, Amber.

Gone But Not Forgotten

AN ONLY CHILD, VALERIE WANTED A SISTER MORE THAN ANY-thing in the world. She never did get one, but in college she met Michelle—the closest thing to a sister she would ever find. They hit it off immediately, as if they had known each other all their lives. They shared each other's hopes, dreams, and fears and vowed always to be there for each other, no matter what!

They partied and dated through their early 20s and talked about how much fun it would be to marry and have children at the same time. It was part of their master plan.

While at Fordham University in the Bronx, they both entered the health profession. They double dated, rarely disagreed, and never judged each other—until, that is, Michelle started dating a jealous and obsessive guy who treated her badly. Though Valerie tried to keep her mouth shut, finally she had to say something.

"There's something scary about him that I don't like," Valerie said. "He has a bad temper and I'm afraid he's going to hurt you."

Michelle told Valerie she appreciated her concern, but assured her that she had his jealousy under control. "We've discussed it," Michelle said. "He's okay."

But Valerie was still unsure. She didn't like his jealous behavior. Michelle was beautiful, men loved her, and she used to flirt and have fun.

But all that stopped when she met this guy. In fact, she became so paranoid of his irrational suspicions that she would prep Valerie about what she could and could not say around him.

The stress took a toll on their friendship, but nothing could sever the ties. They had vowed to be friends until the end; they had crossed their hearts on that. And when Michelle finally dumped him, their friendship blossomed once again.

After college, the two friends went to work at Einstein Hospital in the Bronx. Michelle worked in the clinic and Valerie worked on the maternity floor. And that eerie boyfriend? He had been replaced by another guy who Michelle swore was a keeper.

"This is the one," she said. And he was.

Valerie also met the man of her dreams. Michelle was Valerie's maid of honor at her wedding and Valerie was Michelle's matron of honor. Just like they had dreamed. They were as close as sisters, maybe even closer, because they had the freedom to choose each other, accepting the good and bad qualities each possessed. Their husbands adored them and treated them like African queens and they marveled at their blessing. Who would have believed they would marry and still stay such good friends?

Yet, their friendship came to a screeching halt on February 6, 1996, when Valerie received the worst call of her life. Michelle was dead. Her old boyfriend from college, the only person they had ever disagreed about, harbored anger and hatred against her for the past seven years. He had finally cracked and fatally stabbed Michelle eight times.

"My best friend was dead," Valerie cried. "And there was nothing I could do. What hurt me most was that Michelle always gave of herself to everyone. Although it's been nearly three years, it seems as if it were yesterday. I still remember walking slowly up to her casket. Her mother buried her in a peach dress that I had given her a week before her death. We planned to have kids together and grow old. Now I have to do that alone and she will never know what it will be like to be a mother."

Valerie never got a chance to tell Michelle her good news. She was pregnant. Valerie gave birth to a baby boy, eight months after Michelle's funeral. "I think my son has Michelle's spirit," Valerie always says. "Sometimes I think God sent him to me as a way of replacing her."

Though Michelle has passed on, her memories live forever in Valerie. They kept their promise to each other and remained friends until the very end, though it came much too soon.

A Helping Hand

JEWEL HAD ONE OF THE BUSIEST DAYS IN HER LIFE. AFTER putting her children on the school bus in the morning she rushed off to work. Jewel had to make a presentation to potential clients. She arrived at the office on time only to realize she forgot the report on the kitchen table. So Jewel had to get back in the car and drive home, grab the report, and dash out the door again. She thought she would make it in time, but as soon as she got on the highway her car died. Jewel turned the ignition, stepped on the gas, but the car would not turn over. Her cellular phone wasn't charged, so she couldn't call for help. She stood on the side of the highway, but nobody stopped. Jewel's heart raced; she knew she would be late for the meeting.

"Damn!" she said, looking at her watch. "I can't believe this is happening to me. Not today."

Jewel got back in the car and sat with her head pressed against the wheel. Next thing she knew there was a knock on the window. Jewel looked up to see a woman.

"Are you okay?" the stranger asked.

"My car broke down and I am late for a very important appointment," Jewel said. "Do you have a phone in your car?"

"No," she replied. "But I do have a tank full of gas. Let me take you somewhere."

"But my job is about five miles away," Jewel said. "Are you sure you don't mind?"

"No problem," she said matter-of-factly.

Jewel climbed into the woman's car and they jetted off to her job. On the way, they had a chance to talk—both had young kids, hectic schedules, and businessmen husbands who spent a lot of time on the road. Jewel tried to give the woman a few dollars for gas to show her appreciation, but the woman refused.

"You can do me one favor," the woman said. "Promise to reach out and help someone else in need. Then tell that person to do the same. The chain reaction means more to me than any amount of money."

"Deal," said Jewel. "Thanks so much for your help. I feel as if I know you so well and we just met. Thanks for being a friend to me even though you didn't know me."

"I'm just glad I could help," the woman said, driving off with a beep and wave.

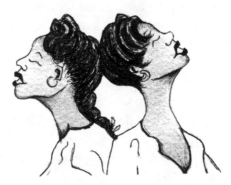

Living by Faith

CAYMAN WAS THE YOUNGEST OF EIGHT CHILDREN, SO IT WAS hard for her to get any attention from her mother or siblings. Cayman was sent to a Catholic school and kept very much to herself.

Sister Rosa, a nun at the school, worried about Cayman and asked her why she was so quiet and shy in class. Cayman just shrugged. As time passed, however, Cayman began to trust Sister Rosa. Soon they started to talk about school, family, and what it meant to be a black Catholic. Cayman had never felt so special before and she and Rosa formed a special bond. Rosa encouraged Cayman to study hard and convinced her to take college prep classes.

"You are much smarter than you think," Sister Rosa would tell Cayman. "Go to college. Reach for the stars." And Cayman did. She got accepted to college and graduated from high school with honors. Sister Rosa attended a family gathering in Cayman's honor. She was just as proud as Cayman's family, for she had truly made a positive impact on her student's life. And she felt like family herself.

Cayman and Sister Rosa kept in touch during Cayman's first year of college, but eventually they lost touch. When Sister Rosa transferred to another school the nuns were unable to forward Cayman's letters and they lost all contact. The friends missed each other terribly but went on with their lives. But the day before Cayman's college graduation, she stopped by the chapel and prayed for guidance, love, her family's health, and that she would be able to communicate with Sister Rosa again. The next thing she knew, Sister Rosa was standing at the door of the chapel. It was like a miracle.

"What are you doing here?" Cayman beamed.

"I wouldn't have missed this for the world," Sister Rosa said.

"But how did you know where to find me?" Cayman asked, perplexed.

"God led me to you twelve years ago," Sister Rosa said. "And God led me back to you again."

Cayman and Sister Rosa hugged and then held hands and prayed together. They thanked God for bringing them back together and vowed to never lose each other again. Even though we may drift apart from our friends from time to time, our faith tells us that we will come face-to-face again. Cayman and Sister Rosa lived by their faith.

In a Tight Situation

$\mathcal{N}$ITA AND CHRISTY WERE ROOMMATES. THE TWO CAREER women in their 20s knew what it meant to be close friends because they were in and out of each other's space as they shared a two-bedroom apartment in the Georgetown area of Washington, D.C. Christy was a nurse at a popular Washington OB-GYN practice and Nita was a television news assistant.

Though they always stuck together, their friendship was really tested the morning Christy woke up to a frantic roommate who couldn't remove a contraceptive sponge from her vagina. Nita struggled to locate the string. "Damn," she said after several tries. "I can't seem to get this sponge out."

Christy went to the garbage to fish out the box in order to read the directions. Nita grew frustrated and a bit nervous. Her boyfriend and a group of their friends were on their way over to the apartment to watch the Super Bowl game and there was still a lot to do around the house.

"Let's call the help line," Christy said, trying to figure out why the directions didn't help. "If there's a number on the box, this must have happened before."

"Oh great," Nita laughed. "The first time Lance and I have sex and the whole world will know about it."

The woman who answered the phone at the help line instructed Nita to fill the tub halfway with warm water and sit for about 10 minutes. She did it, but still could not get a grip on the sponge's string. The doorbell rang—a couple of Nita's girlfriends showed up early. The friends laughed hysterically at the thought of taking Nita to the emergency room to have the sponge removed.

"I can see us now," said one friend. "Excuse me, doctor, but our friend has a little problem."

Nita and her girlfriends laughed until tears came to their eyes, each friend making jokes as Nita struggled to get serious. Before long, Nita was surrounded by four girlfriends, all trying to comfort her in between the giggles.

"Call Lance," Nita told Christy. "Tell him I have a little problem."

Lance came over right away. He was surprised and embarrassed that the whole peanut gallery had gathered to witness the "sponge incident." Everyone left the room and Lance tried to pull it out, but he couldn't.

"We just might have to take you to the hospital, baby," Lance mused. "This could only happen to us."

After the friends heard Nita and Lance laughing, they reappeared in Nita's bedroom. One had a pair of scissors. One had tweezers. One had a knife. Another had tongs. They were laughing and getting sillier by the minute. Nita tried not to laugh, but it was impossible. Her friends stood around the room trying to come up with a solution, then one of the friends suggested that Christy get it out.

"Not me," Christy said. "Nita is my girl and everything, but I can't go there."

The girlfriends could not contain their laughter. In fact,

two of the girls were on the floor holding their stomachs. Suddenly, Nita got serious. She looked at Christy in a way that only roommates could understand and asked for her help.

"If you can help with the examination of total strangers, then you should be able to help me," Nita pleaded. "Pleeease, roomy. Please help me."

Christy didn't want to do it, but she knew Nita was ready for the ordeal to end. She went into the medicine chest and grabbed a pair of latex gloves. It took some doing, but Christy was able to remove the sponge. Lance and the friends applauded as Christy tossed it in the trash can.

"Ease up the next time," Christy told Lance. "Don't make this a habit."

The girlfriends laughed again. Then Nita sat up and made her friends promise they would never tell a living soul the sponge story.

"Not your boyfriend. Not your mama. Not even your husband when you get one," Nita begged. "I mean nobody. You can't tell anybody. This stays between us."

They agreed it would be their little secret; they would never tell a soul. So instead of being interviewed, one of Nita's friends wrote this story down for me. To this day, every time one of the girlfriends hears the word *sponge,* she laughs and thinks about Nita.

Eighty and Proud of It

SOME GIRLFRIENDS WOULD RATHER HAVE A TOOTH PULLED without Novocain than reveal their age or weight to anyone. My friend Evelyn used to be one of those women. You see, she had been a reporter for the *Pittsburgh Courier* before it was popular for black women to work in journalism. She covered Malcolm X, Martin Luther King, Jr., and even Willie Mays. Evelyn wrote stories on the lynchings in the South and got arrested with a group of protesters after she tucked away her pen, pad, and press credentials and joined a demonstration.

I love talking to Evelyn and listening to her many stories of yesteryear. As black women in a field that has always been dominated by white men, Evelyn and I quickly bonded. Our experiences in journalism were so similiar that our age difference didn't seem to matter. Evelyn is just another one of the girls, as far as I am concerned. During one of our many conversations, Evelyn told me she was born in Elizabeth City, North Carolina, and how quickly her parents moved her and her brother up north when she announced at 4 years old that she wanted to pick cotton when she grew up.

"You wanted to pick cotton?" I asked Evelyn in a tone filled with disbelief. Over the years, Evelyn and I had talked about a lot of things, but when she talked about picking cotton it really dawned on me that she was indeed an elder stateswoman. In that same conversation, Evelyn told me about the day she turned 80. It was a milestone for her because it was the first time she let anyone know how old she was.

"I called up my closest friends and invited them to my house for a birthday luncheon," Evelyn said. "We sat there talking and eating and then I made my big announcement. I am 80 years old—they were shocked."

With Evelyn taking ballet lessons, traveling the world, sitting on more than a dozen boards, and attending every major function in the city, her friends couldn't believe an 80-year-old woman could look that good.

Evelyn believes that keeping busy is the key to her energy. When it comes to networking and being a good friend, Evelyn wins hands down. She is so worldly and gracious that she can mingle with women of all ages, and if she finds something in you that she likes, then you have a friend for life. At my baby shower, Evelyn told everyone that she's my senior citizen friend. I feel so blessed that Evelyn Cunningham considers me one of her girlfriends.

Friendship & Fame

Sistah Girlfriends
Separated at Birth

When the Queen of Talk, Oprah Winfrey, needs some-one to talk to, she calls Gayle.

That's Gayle King—a broadcast journalist turned talk show host who just happens to be Oprah's best friend, confidante, and sistah-girlfriend. Although Oprah has always talked about Gayle on her show, and even had Gayle's mother and ex-husband on two different *Oprah* shows, few had ever seen Gayle until the friends appeared on a prime-time show about friendship in 1989. I was a reporter at a New Jersey paper back then and I had a chance to interview Gayle.

"A lot of people think I don't really exist," Gayle told me. "I remember attending a speaking engagement with Oprah and the audience was shocked when Oprah asked me to stand up. I guess they thought I was make believe."

Gayle is indeed real. In fact, my best friend Linda Taylor and I had a chance to meet Oprah and Gayle during a taping in New York. They were so pleasant and sweet that Linda and I wanted to be their friends, too!

Gayle told me that she and Oprah met in 1976 while they worked at WJZ-TV in Baltimore. Oprah was an anchor-woman and Gayle was an entry-level production assistant.

There was a snowstorm one night and Oprah invited Gayle to crash at her apartment instead of driving home to Washington, D.C. Gayle was surprised by the invitation because of the differences in their positions, but they shared a special bond—both were black women and both were journalists.

"I didn't have a toothbrush, undies, or anything," Gayle remembered. "I was reluctant at first, but Oprah said not to worry because she had all that stuff. We stayed up talking all night and ate lunch together the next day."

That was more than 20 years ago. Their friendship has survived career moves, King's marriage and divorce and reunion and breakup, Stedman and the occasional man in Oprah's life before him, not to mention three-figure phone bills. When I called Gayle about this book, she called me back right away; she seemed to remember the day she introduced Linda and me to Oprah. Well, the first thing I wanted to know was whether her entry into the talk show world had caused a rift between the two high-profile friends.

"There is no rivalry," Gayle insisted. "We are not competitive friends. We want what's best for the other. Our taping schedule is the same, but we are never on at the same time. I don't want to get my butt kicked. In fact, Oprah has been very helpful. She had her staff come up with some show ideas for me—that's the kind of friend Oprah is."

Gayle said Oprah has always been more than generous, showering her with all kinds of lavish gifts. Gayle's favorite gift was a nanny. "I called Oprah and told her that I was pregnant with my second child. I was crying and carrying on. Then Oprah asked me if I was finished. Then she proceeded to tell me that I make her sick with all my tears. Then about a week later, Oprah called me back and said she had a great idea for a baby gift. I was thinking about a double crib or double stroller and Oprah said she was going to set me up with a nanny. She said she was going to establish the Gayle King Nanny Fund and put enough money in it for a nanny and renovations to my raised ranch-style home. She said it would make the house more comfortable for everybody."

A good vacation to Gayle is "packing up my kids, bikes, and the dog and driving to Martha's Vineyard, like the Beverly Hillbillies. Oprah's idea of a vacation is chartering a yacht and taking her friends on a cruise to San Tropez."

When Gayle's marriage failed, it was her buddy, doctor Oprah Winfrey, who helped her get through her divorce. Gayle said Oprah has always been there in times of trouble. It was Oprah who delivered the eulogy at Gayle's mother's funeral a few years back. Gayle told me it's really hard for her to focus on one aspect of her girlfriend's personality because she is just an all-around good person.

Though Oprah is the queen of TV, Gayle told me a little secret. She said Oprah never watches TV. So the night O.J. took the infamous white Bronco ride down a California highway, Gayle called Oprah and told her she had to turn on the tube. They watched the chase in shock.

"We stayed on the phone the whole time," Gayle said. "Both of us were at a loss for words that night. We couldn't believe it. Not O.J.! We wanted to know where he was going and how the chase was going to end. We were really afraid that he was going to kill himself. And when the chase ended, we stayed on the phone even longer trying to make sense of it all."

Some say the two women might have been separated at birth—they walk alike, talk alike, and even finish each other's sentences. I believe it could be true. While interviewing Gayle for *Just Between Girlfriends*, I couldn't believe how much she and Oprah sounded alike. What was even funnier to me was that Linda and I have been friends so long that we sometimes sound alike, too. Guess it's just something about best friends.

Despite the Oprah mania, TV ratings, and Emmy awards, Gayle says her best friend is just a regular person and great friend.

"I attended an engagement with Oprah and wondered why six policemen were there to direct traffic and keep the crowd orderly. I wondered who was coming," Gayle recalled. "I thought all the fuss was over Diana Ross or Michael Jackson, and it took me back a bit when I realized it was all for my friend."

The friendship shared by Oprah and Gayle is sweet and genuine, grounded in honesty and love. Gayle says they are silly when they get together and love to laugh. With their busy schedules, the friends really have to make a point of spending time together. Gayle and her children recently spent the weekend in Philadelphia with Oprah as she acted in the movie *Beloved*.

"It wasn't enough for us to just be there," Gayle laughed. "Oprah made us extras in a crowd scene. It was so much fun."

Though the friends have a lot to laugh about, Gayle admits that she knows all the secrets and inside scoop about Oprah. She said she'd rather have her tongue cut out than betray her best friend, and I feel the same way about my best friend Linda, who was married to New York Giants football star Lawrence "LT" Taylor.

When I interviewed Gayle the first time around, I realized her friendship with Oprah is just like the friendship I share with Linda. Gayle told me that she and Oprah sometimes run out of things to say and hang up only to call 15 minutes later to ask what the other is doing. Linda and I do the same thing. When Gayle told me that she and her husband divorced, I couldn't help but think of Linda again because she and LT were divorced around the same time.

"I have other friends, but none like Oprah," Gayle lamented. "It's rare to find a friend who is loyal and can be trusted totally. I am very proud to be Oprah's best friend."

The Write Stuff

*C*HANCES ARE THAT WHEN I MENTION DONNA GRANT AND Virginia DeBerry, you immediately think of them as the best-selling authors of *Trying to Sleep in the Bed You Made*. But what you don't know is that those two celebrities owe their success to each other—their friendship. In fact, Donna Grant and Virginia DeBerry had the potential to be enemies. In the early 1980s, they were both young, beautiful, full-figured black models competing for work at the same agency.

In the glamorous world of fashion there were always two blondes, but two black girls didn't stand a chance. So they were constantly competing. If one was working, the other was not. It was that simple.

But Donna and Virginia were not the jealous types and they quickly realized they had a lot more in common than modeling. They both dreamed of becoming entrepreneurs and taking charge of their own futures. Before long, Virginia quit modeling to pursue her dream of becoming an agent, convincing Donna to become her client. Later when Virginia accepted a job at Hanes, she didn't forget about Donna. Virginia immediately pulled Donna into the project, but both women still had bigger dreams.

With each other's support they decided to quit their jobs and start a magazine called *Maxima*. They worked around the clock, camped out on Virginia's living room couch, desperately trying to get the first issue out. This was it, the friends thought. They had finally achieved their dreams. Yet at the peak of their happiness, the backers ran into financial troubles. "We were crushed," Donna said. "It felt like we had been punched in the stomach by the heavyweight champ."

"But we didn't have time to wallow in our pity," both friends said almost in unison.

They had become best friends and refused to give up so easily. This time they took on one of the biggest challenges of all—a book. They tossed around ideas, came up with a story line, and wrote around the clock. To their surprise and delight, the manuscript was soon completed and published.

Inspired by their success, Donna and Virginia decided to do it again. But this time they weren't so lucky. Their second book was never published. Their agent simply couldn't sell it.

But despite their setback they never gave up. They both got full-time jobs again and wrote in their spare time. Then, exactly 10 years after their magazine folded, Donna and Virginia finally achieved their ultimate dream. Their next book, *Trying to Sleep in the Bed You Made*, was published and then quietly soared to the Blackboard Bestseller charts.

"There were days we wanted to jump off a bridge," Virginia said. "But it was the strength from each other that kept us going."

"She's right. We got each other through the valleys," Donna confessed. "We listened to the other. There is a way we trust each other that cannot be explained."

These friends often say they trust each other more than they trust themselves. I guess you can say these two friends have the "write stuff."

Yolanda, Granny, & Shiba

GOSPEL SINGER YOLANDA ADAMS AND HER GRANNY ALWAYS had a close relationship, but they became even closer when Yolanda was 14 years old—that was the year Yolanda's daddy died. The oldest of five siblings, Yolanda knew she had to be strong for them and her mom. Granny knew her oldest granddaughter was in just as much pain as the others, though she put on a brave front.

"Granny instructed me to go straight to the word of God and pray," Yolanda told me. "Granny said I would find strength in the word of God and she was right. She is a woman of few words, but when she speaks you believe her words will be full of wisdom. Granny also makes the best gumbo I ever had."

When it comes to cooking gumbo—well, Granny has shared her recipe with Yolanda, but the songstress said she will stick to what she does best, which is singing to the glory of God.

"My gumbo doesn't come out like Granny's," Yolanda confessed.

And when the lady Granny was living with passed on, Yolanda insisted that she live with her. She didn't want Granny to live alone.

"She prays for me and with me," said Yolanda. "We have a bond that could never be broken. Without a doubt, my Granny really is my best friend."

As Yolanda continues to rise to prominence in the field of

gospel music, it's doubtful that her inner circle will change. She surrounds herself with loving family members and friends, like her manager Shiba Haley.

"Shiba and I have a lot in common," Yolanda said. "And I know she has my best interest at heart all the time, and that's not always the case with managers."

Yolanda said she can relax when Shiba is around, and the two women have a lot of fun together. Yolanda said she shared so many wonderful times with Shiba that it was hard to tell a single story about their friendship, and then something clicked.

"Okay, I remember one of the times we laughed the most in one day," Yolanda recalled. "It was at the taping of an infomercial. It was taped on top of a mountain, over the ocean in California. We had to scale down the cliff to get to location and then hike back up to the top."

Yolanda said it was cold on the mountain. Everyone was bundled up, but Yolanda had to sing and look fabulous in a gown.

"I was freezing," Yolanda said. "I mean I was shivering and trying to get warm and Shiba was standing there smiling with her coat on. She kept trying to encourage me to think warm, but it was impossible. All we could do is laugh about it."

Yolanda said she laughed so hard the makeup artist told her that she was in danger of cracking her makeup. And once Yolanda adjusted to the big chill, the director suggested that she change gowns several times in order to add zest to the production.

"There I was on this mountain trying to change gowns," Yolanda said. "I tried to hide so nobody could see me and Shiba tried to help, but every time we looked at each other we just burst out laughing. We were out there about three hours."

To this day, Yolanda and Shiba laugh about that day on the mountain. "We have a lot of fun together," Yolanda said. "But our friendship is so much more than that. She gives me sound advice and our friendship is based on being truthful to each other."

Yolanda counts her blessings when it comes to her friendship with Granny and Shiba. She loves to sing their praise.

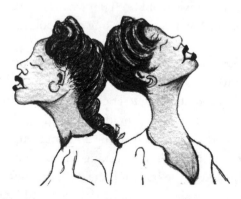

Friends in Harmony

A FEW DAYS BEFORE THEY STARTED CLASSES AT TEMPLE University in Philadelphia, Renee Neufville and Jean Norris met during freshman orientation. After a meeting, they were among a group of young women who went back to someone's room to hang out and get better acquainted. As Renee recalled, somebody was cooking, somebody was doing hair, and the rest of us were talking over tunes on the radio.

Then it happened. Freddie Jackson's song "Nice 'N' Slow" came on and Renee and Jean both began singing out loud. Each looked at the other approvingly and to their surprise they began to sing in harmony.

"We were both like, dang, you can really sing," Renee told me. "And as they say, the rest is history."

From that day forward, Renee and Jean went to the music hall after classes and practiced. Renee played the piano and together they'd sing. They became roommates and between studies Renee and Jean collaborated on songs and entered talent shows.

"We became inseparable," Renee said. "We spent so much time together that we began to sound alike and think alike. We were more like sisters."

Besides being born within four days of each other, they seemed to experience a lot of things at the same time. The duo had their hearts broken at the same time, had solid families, and were very interested in education. Renee said she and Jean bonded over cups of herbal tea and cinnamon raisin toast.

It was over tea that the friends decided that they had won enough talent contests and were ready to take their talent to the next level. Together the songbirds came up with the name Zhane. Rappers D.J. Jazzy Jeff and the Fresh Prince (rapper turned actor Will Smith) heard about them. They sang background for the rappers for a short while, then went to New York to pursue their dream. Renee said they spent hours in various record company executive offices belting out a medley of songs.

Zhane was a big hit with their first singles, "Hey Mr. D.J." and "Groove Thing." Now, instead of playing the talent show circuit, these best friends have played all over the world. In fact, on a recent trip to Japan, Renee and Jean reflected on their journey.

"We stepped out on our faith," Renee said. "We knew we could sing, but at the core of it all we became best friends. We are the key to each other's success. For us, it's our love of music and the gift of song that makes our friendship so special."

Every Woman's Girlfriend

THE LATE DR. BETTY SHABAZZ, CORETTA SCOTT KING, AND Myrlie Evers-Willams became friends and sisters through their husbands' struggle to improve conditions for black Americans. While most brides make a vow to love in sickness and health, these women also made a commitment to stand by the men they married even though that meant in the face of constant adversity and even danger.

It was their husbands' fight to bring equality, justice, and self-respect to black Americans that left these women and mothers widowed. They were all young when their husbands were brutally cut down by bullets at the hands of people who did not like what they stood for. They shared a bond that was forged by the assassination of their husbands, and these girlfriends understood the pain and agony that goes with losing their spouses.

But tragedy struck again for the three girlfriends when Dr. Shabazz, widow of Malcolm X, died on June 23, 1997. Dr. Shabazz was burned over 85 percent of her body in a fire set by her own grandson. Days before Dr. Shabazz's death, Myrlie and Coretta rushed to her bedside. I covered the story for the *Daily News*. They said they didn't know if their friend Betty could see or hear them, but they wanted to be there to support her. These friends had long found strength and comfort in their very special bond and appeared to have found tranquility in each other. In fact, the day they visited Betty in the hospital, the three friends were supposed to be in Miami for a private retreat.

Myrlie and Coretta found it hard to hold back the tears and they were not alone. For many African-American women, myself included, Dr. Shabazz was the epitome of womanhood. She was a beacon of strength, dignity, beauty, and determination. I had the opportunity to meet Dr. Shabazz three weeks before her death. She had read my first book, *Mama Knows Best,* and invited me to be a guest on her WLIB radio talk show. I was thrilled when I received the invitation and in awe when we met. As a reporter, I've interviewed many celebrities, but this was the first time a celebrity interviewed me. Dr. Shabazz sensed how nervous I was and started talking about her own pregnancies in order to break the ice. She had quickly taken a liking to me and the feeling was mutual. Dr. Shabazz wanted to know more about me, my son, Jordan, and my life as a single mother, just like her.

Dr. Shabazz and I laughed a lot that day. She shared her recipe for oven-fried chicken and encouraged me to be a role model for my son. "Lead by example," she told me. The conversation was deep and at the same time extremely heartwarming. It was a conversation between a new mom and a worldly mother who had been there, done that. All too soon, my radio time was up. I was so excited about meeting Dr. Shabazz that I told everyone about it. When I received a call a few weeks later from the Daily News City Desk with news of Shabazz's death, I too cried. Like Myrlie Evers-Willams and

Coretta Scott King, I felt as if I had lost a dear friend. Dr. Shabazz had that kind of effect on people, whether they were longtime friends or newer friends, like me, who she had collected along the way. Dr. Shabazz was every woman's girl-friend and the example she set will live on through us all.

Linda & Me

I WAS NEVER A BIG FOOTBALL FAN; IN FACT, I STILL DON'T REALLY understand the game all that well. But it was at Giants Stadium that I met my best friend, Linda Taylor. She was the wife of Lawrence "LT" Taylor, the New York Giants superstar who has been called the greatest NFL linebacker of all times. I was the girlfriend of another Giants linebacker at the time.

When I arrived in the wives' section of the stands, there was a woman in my seat. I showed her my ticket, but she was reluctant to move. She told me that "the wives" sit anywhere they want and pointed to another seat for me. I didn't want to do it, but she forced me to put her in her place. She quickly moved. At halftime, she proceeded to tell the other wives about the incident and I suddenly became an outcast. Then I walked into the bathroom and there was Linda, draped in a full-length black mink coat with a matching hat and muff. The way everyone swarmed around her, I knew she had to be Mrs. LT. I complimented her on her outfit and she laughed out loud. Linda opened her coat and let me in on a secret. She had on jeans and a pajama top, with a sweater over it. We stood in the bathroom together laughing like old friends, though we hadn't even really met.

We introduced ourselves and laughed at the fact that we were both there to cheer for linebackers. There was something very comforting about Linda from the start. I took a chance, but I told her what happened in the wives' section and she laughed.

"I'm glad you told her," Linda said. "Her husband hasn't been off the bench all season."

We laughed again. Then Linda invited me to sit with her. I was delighted. Though she was an avid fan, we talked and giggled most of the game. Linda and I exchanged numbers, but we didn't see each other until the next home game, which was two weeks later. We both apologized for not calling, but we didn't have time to talk on that day because we both had friends with us. For the rest of the season, Linda always had friends and family with her. We always spoke, but never had time to catch up. The season ended and I returned to Northeastern University in Boston.

When the football season came back around, Linda was pleasantly surprised that I was still in the picture. I was shocked to see that she was pregnant with her third child. We hugged and kissed and again promised to get together. Almost overnight, the relationship with my linebacker became shaky and reports began to surface that her linebacker had a drug problem. One Sunday, instead of going to the game, we both ended up at Mt. Olive Baptist Church.

A couple of weeks later, Linda called me at work to tell me she had a baby girl, who she named Paula. On my lunch break, I went to visit her. Linda seemed a little troubled, and I was completely devastated that my linebacker decided we should see other people. As our men celebrated a shot at the championship, we shared our disappointment in them and made a pledge to "get a life." Two weeks later, Linda and I were on our way to a party. As we drove, we talked about our problems, our lives, and our families. Through our tears, we made an unspoken pact to always be there for each other. That was 12 years ago. We've been best friends ever since.

Linda held my hand as I struggled to make my mark in journalism, talked me out of marrying a complete idiot, and laughed hysterically the night I table danced on a dare (after too many shots of tequila).

I comforted Linda through her separation and divorce, cried at the thought of us being apart when she moved to Charlotte, and still talk to her on the telephone almost every day. We love each other's children like we both gave birth to them, and we want the very best for each other.

We laugh every time we think back to the night we snuck into a private party at Eddie Murphy's house, the wonderful time we had at New York Knick Charles Oakley's 29th birthday, and the many pool parties we had at Linda's house.

When it comes to our friendship, we accept the good and the bad in each other. Sure, we've had a few disagreements over the years, but we've never betrayed each other's trust. We find comfort in knowing that our most intimate secrets will always remain safely tucked away. We have a bond that could never, ever be broken. Although Linda has taught me a lot over the years, she never did teach me the rules of football. Every time I watch a football game, I think back to that day at Giants Stadium when my best friend entered my life.

Star Quality

THERE WAS A SEA OF AFRICAN-AMERICAN WOMEN WEARING pink and green clothing at the Alpha Kappa Alpha Sorority Inc. boule in Los Angeles. TV personality Star Jones, who was on the sorority's national board, had just finished listening to actress Vanessa Bell Calloway, also a soror, deliver the keynote address. Star enjoyed the speech so much that she decided to introduce herself to Vanessa.

The women became engaged in a conversation that was so enjoyable they decided to ditch the next boule program and go to the movies.

"It was a bond that I had never felt with any other woman," Star told me. "We were like sisters in an hour. I have a sister, so I know that closeness, and it came immediately with Vanessa."

They remained close. And when Star made the transition from Brooklyn assistant district attorney to Court TV, Vanessa helped Star negotiate her contract and gave her tips on what she should avoid and amend. Vanessa also told Star, a newcomer in the world of television and entertainment, to "treat everyone in the business as if they are the president of the company because you never know where people may end up."

Star, who moved to Los Angeles for her Court TV job, was there for the birth of Vanessa's daughters, Ashley and Alexander, and remembers pleading with the nurse to give Vanessa some painkillers, though Vanessa had made up her mind to have natural childbirth.

"Give my girlfriend something for the pain," Star remembered, yelling at the top of her lungs. "I was out of control. In between contractions, Vanessa had to tell me to calm down and relax, like I was the one giving birth."

After a rough delivery, Vanessa caught up on her sleep while Auntie Star caressed baby Alexander in her arms. Star stayed at the hospital with Vanessa most of the day to help comfort her girlfriend.

"We need girlfriends," Star said, adding that she and Vanessa are also friends with actress Lela Rochon. "The three of us have a bond that will last forever. We depend on each other and have a loyalty that is unspoken."

Star had become such a popular analyst on Court TV that she landed her own show, *Jones & Jury,* and covered the O.J. Simpson trial for *Inside Edition.* Covering the Simpson trial was Star's biggest challenge. Though it was widely considered that other journalists and attorneys had crossed the line from analyzing the facts, Star would not express her personal opinion about the double murder case.

"There were days when I was almost in tears," Star confessed. "I was getting pressure from *Inside Edition* to get an interview with O.J. As a lawyer I had the pressure of knowing what the evidence was. My only stake in it all was my desire to be fair. In many ways I was overwhelmed."

Star confided her most intimate feelings and opinions about the trial and its coverage to Vanessa and Lela. The actresses were so busy helping Star sort out her feelings, they never bothered to give their take on the case. When Star finished sharing her position, Vanessa reminded Star of a lesson that both their families had always lived by:

"To thine own self be true," Vanessa whispered with confidence. "If you can look in the mirror and smile every morning, you know you've done the right thing and you should feel good about yourself."

Obviously, Star Jones did something right because she has since gained the attention of Ms. TV News herself, Barbara Walters. Now, Star is a commentator on Barbara's new daytime show, *The View*.

"My girlfriends helped me get through the hardest time I faced professionally," Star told me. "That's what friendship is all about—being able to depend on your home girls, no matter what."

Foxy's Friend

AFTER PERFORMING FOR SOLD-OUT AUDIENCES ACROSS THE country, teenage rapper Foxy Brown finds comfort in spending downtime with R&B singer Monica, who is just as young and successful as herself. The teens expressed interest in meeting each other after finding out they were both about the same age. Monica lives in Atlanta, so after Foxy performed there their managers arranged for them to hook up.

They clicked immediately. Foxy says it had something to do with the fact that both teenagers were able to perform with the maturity and conviction of grown women. They were both old souls.

"This business is tough," Foxy told me. "We are kids in an adult arena. Everybody needs somebody to talk to and I enjoy talking to Monica. We talk almost every day."

What do these teenage stars talk about? You know—the same things you talked about when you were their age—boyfriends.

"We are both dating someone in the business," Foxy said. "We cry on each other's shoulder. My girl Monica is mature beyond her years. She's an old soul and gives me advice about dating a celebrity. She will stay on the phone for hours schooling me and making me feel better about my relationship. Then a few days later, she'll call me back crying with the same problem and I have to give her some of her own advice."

And when they are not talking about the fellas, these girl-friends can be found shopping. "In Atlanta we hit Lennox Mall. In L.A. we do Rodeo Drive," Foxy said. "We do normal things like other young women our age. The only difference is that we have jobs that put us in the spotlight."

Teammates & Friends

DEBBIE MILLER-PALMORE ALWAYS LOVED TO PLAY BASKETball. She played in high school, college, and on the U.S. Olympic team. So it wasn't a surprise when she decided to go overseas to play in England. Debbie had never been there before, but she was eager to play women's basketball at the professional level. And she wanted to play for an English-speaking country.

One of the first people Debbie met was her teammate, Gracelyn Williams. They had more in common than basketball—they were both black, physical education teachers, and they both went to church regularly. They spent three years together traveling the world, including Italy, Scotland, Ireland, and Germany, while playing basketball. It was Gracelyn who turned Debbie on to tea. In England everyone drinks tea—all the time.

"Grace and I bonded on the road," Debbie said. "There's something about being on a team that brings people together. I was away from home and she had lived in England for a while. I felt comfort in knowing that her family was nearby."

After Debbie returned to the United States, the teammates kept in touch. They talk for hours over a cup of tea. I talked to Gracelyn and she summed up her friendship with Debbie by simply saying, "We're more than teammates, we're mates."

Count on Me

GRAMMY AWARD–WINNING SINGERS CECE WINANS AND Whitney Houston have found comfort in calling each other girlfriend. Their beautiful voices brought them together, but their love for each other keeps their friendship alive. They've become so close, their relationship is more like kin. CeCe was a bridesmaid in Whitney's wedding and she's the godmother of her daughter.

CeCe often tells people that God sent Whitney her way and Whitney says their friendship was a "spontaneous" bond. CeCe performed at *It's Showtime at the Apollo* a while back and I was there to interview her for the New Jersey newspaper I worked for. I remember being upstairs in CeCe's dressing room when Whitney dropped by to say hello. They were very excited to see each other—hugged and kissed each other. I was so impressed by their display of love. CeCe convinced Whitney to go on stage to say hello to the crowd. Whitney was dressed down and had on a hat, so the audience didn't believe it was Whitney, until she suddenly started to sing.

It was through song that Whitney and CeCe's friendship began and continues to flourish. The two have often worked with each other on singing projects and seem to enjoy sharing the spotlight with each other. They sang about the strength of their own friendship when they sang the single "Count On Me," on the *Waiting to Exhale* soundtrack. They sang: "Count on me through thick and thin."

Jurnee's Jazz

*C*HILD ACTRESS JURNEE SMOLLET, WHO PLAYED THE LEAD role in last year's hit movie, *Eve's Bayou*, is only 11 years old, but when it comes to friendship it's her big sister Jazz who she calls her best friend.

"Jazz is my best friend," Jurnee told me. "She is a great sister and she is always there to help me out. Jazz and my mom make me feel so good and they are very loving. They are happy when I do something good and tell me when I am doing something wrong."

Jurnee said she has a lot of friends at her Los Angeles private school who want to know all about her adventures as a child star, but when she wants to discuss something important with a friend she looks for Jazz.

"Jazz, Mommy, and I have girls' night out," said Jurnee. "That means we go shopping, swimming, play basketball, and have sleep overs right on our living room floor. Jazz and Mommy make me feel very special, even though I am one of six children."

Flipping Out Together

GYMNAST DOMINIQUE DAWES FLIPPED HER WAY INTO THE hearts of Americans when she helped bring home the Gold during the 1996 Summer Olympics in Atlanta. Being in the spotlight was nothing new for Dominique; she's been a gymnast most of her life.

When she was 14 years old, Dominique and her friend Crystal Bennett trained at a private gymnast club in Silver Springs, Maryland. While there one day, they met another gymnast named Umme Salim. There was something about Umme that Dominique and Crystal liked, so the three quickly became friends.

"We had a lot in common," Dominique told me. "We liked going to the mall, dancing, and working out. In a short amount of time we became inseparable."

Dominique and Umme continued to practice and compete in gymnastics and Crystal became a cheerleader. Dominique said she secretly always wanted to become a cheerleader, but her hectic gymnastic schedule didn't permit it. So one Halloween, Dominique and Umme borrowed Crystal's extra cheerleading uniforms and the three friends set out for the mall—all dressed as cheerleaders.

To Dominique's surprise, the cute little outfits and pompoms were a magnet for the guys. They were attracting more guys than they knew what to do with. After about an hour of flirting and talking to guys, the girlfriends were approached by "some real cute guys."

"They asked if we could do a flip," Dominique recalled.

"Can *we* flip?" Umme asked with a touch of sarcasm.

Dominique and Umme handed their pom-poms to Crystal and the two gymnasts put on the performance of a lifetime.

"We flipped all the way down the mall without stopping," Dominique laughed. "We actually flipped from one end of the mall to the other. Those guys couldn't believe it—their mouths were wide open. They wanted to know if we could teach them how to do it."

Dominique and Umme never did tell the guys they were gymnasts who had spent years developing their skills.

"It was our little practical joke," Dominique said. "Umme and I still laugh about it to this day."

We Were Only Fifteen

ACTRESS DEBBI MORGAN, WHO WILL GO DOWN IN SOAP-opera history for her role as Dr. Angie Hubbard on *All My Children*, says she and her girlfriend Vanessa Townsend will always share a special friendship.

Debbi and Vanessa both attended Catholic school in Manhattan. The girlfriends had a lot in common, especially their love of junk food, particularly sweets. Almost every day they would stop off for sundaes, candy, or donuts. So the day Vanessa scarfed down nearly a pack of Oreo cookies and about ten White Castle hamburgers, Debbi didn't give it a second thought.

They were two weeks away from finishing their sophomore year. Debbi thought Vanessa's appetite was simply part of the excitement of summer vacation. After school ended for the summer, the girlfriends lost touch for a few weeks—they were not from the same neighborhood. Then Debbi received a call from Vanessa.

"She wanted to get together," Debbi recalled. "I was a little busy and said we could do it soon. Vanessa explained that she really wanted to see me. She told me that she was in the hospital. I wanted to know what was wrong with her."

Debbi said there was a very long pause and Vanessa said she was pregnant. Debbi began to cry.

"It was as if it had happened to me," Debbi said. "I was confused and angry because she was my best friend and she hadn't shared her situation with me. I didn't really know what to say, but I knew it had to be tough."

Vanessa was not really in the hospital; she was at a home for pregnant teenagers. Debbi wanted to visit immediately, but Vanessa had to get approval from the staff of the home. Once the details were worked out, Debbi went to see her friend. When Vanessa walked through the door, her stomach was popped since she was in her ninth month of pregnancy, and Debbi cried again when she saw her.

"It was very emotional for me," Debbi said. "We were kids, only 15 years old. I put my arms around Vanessa as she told me that the nuns would not let her come back to school unless she gave the baby up for adoption. I told her to give the baby up so we could graduate together."

Vanessa made Debbi cross her heart and promise never to tell, but she planned to keep her baby. Vanessa said she was going to pretend that she gave the baby up so that the nuns would let her finish school, but she would really keep it.

Less than a week later, Vanessa gave birth to a little boy. She named him Brian. Vanessa followed her plan, just like she said. Debbi kept Vanessa's secret and never told a soul. Debbi also did what she could to help Vanessa with the baby.

"It was so funny to see Vanessa with a baby," Debbi said. "I got a kick out of watching her with a baby. Vanessa's mother made her live up to her responsibility as a student and a mother. When she needed a break, Vanessa would bring the baby over to my house."

Debbi said the nuns didn't find out about baby Brian until after their graduation and Brian turned out to be a wonderful human being. Though their friendship was established long before baby Brian, Debbi said his birth certainly brought them closer together.

"I wanted to be there for Vanessa," Debbi said. "We've been there for each other ever since. From then until now, we share in each other's excitement and disappointment. Whatever happens to one of us, happens to both of us."

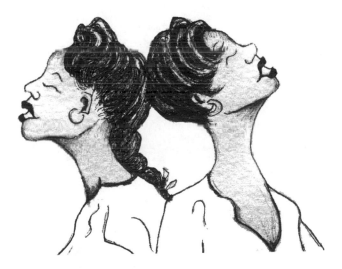

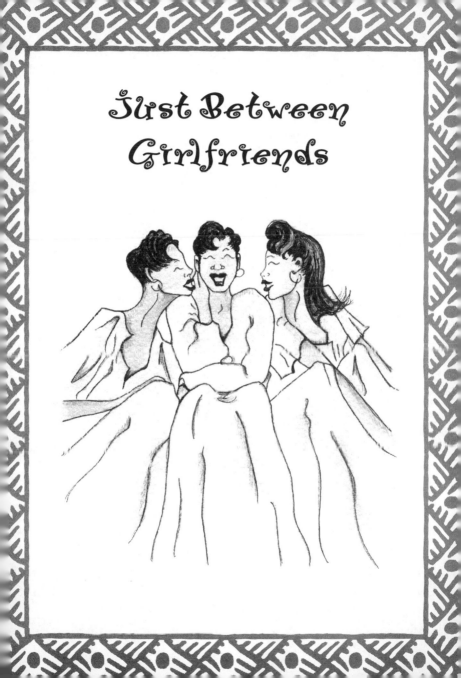

The Strength of a Friend

RHONDA AND SHARI MET AS NEIGHBORS, BUT OVER THE years they became the very best of friends. They saw each other every day and spoke on the telephone at least twice a day. They were suburban moms who took turns carpooling their sons to basketball, soccer, baseball, and swimming practice—and even an occasional date when they became teenagers.

"If you take them, I will pick them up," one would say. "That will give you time to make dinner or tape *Oprah* for me."

They had become so close that their husbands and other friends joked that they even started to look and sound alike.

"Is this Rhonda or Shari?" people asked when they called either house.

Between them, there were no secrets. Like the day Rhonda confessed that she dreaded the thought of getting old and she had noticed that her hair was graying and thinning out already. Shari reminded her that it was just a part of life and she should be lucky she had lived long enough to experience it.

So when Rhonda found an upsetting letter in her 16-year-old son's shirt pocket as she did the laundry, she immediately called Shari.

"Come over quick," Rhonda said, as she slammed down the phone.

In a flash, Shari walked through the door. "What's wrong?"

"Read this," Rhonda replied as she handed her girlfriend a piece of crumpled looseleaf paper. The neatly written letter was from her son's girlfriend. She hadn't gotten her period and believed she was pregnant.

"His life is over," Rhonda cried. "I had such high hopes for my son and now his life is over. He's just a baby himself."

Shari froze. Shari considered Rhonda's son as her own; this was just as alarming for her. Shari wiped Rhonda's tears and hugged her.

"Don't worry, honey," Shari said, fighting back her own tears. "We'll get through this. Everything will be all right. Everything will be okay. Don't worry, honey."

"His girlfriend is already two months pregnant and she wants the baby," Rhonda cried. "Why would a 15-year-old girl want to take on such a big responsibility when she is just a child herself? What are we going to do?"

"We're going to call her mother right now," Shari said matter-of-factly.

"I can't," Rhonda replied. "I'll cry, and besides, my son will hate me if he finds out I was snooping through his clothes."

"Snooping my ass," Shari shot back. "You were washing the clothes, and the last time I checked you and your husband pay all the bills in this house, which means all its contents belong to you. Technically, this is your shirt."

Even in the midst of a crisis, the friends stopped to laugh. It was the kind of comic relief Shari knew her friend needed at that moment. After the laughter came more tears. Rhonda didn't know how she would tell her husband.

"You don't have to tell him," Shari said. "We are going to handle this, mama to mama. Now give me that child's number so I can call her mama."

"You?"

"Yes, me," Shari said. "You are in no shape to handle this. I'll simply pretend I'm you."

Rhonda handed over the number and Shari dialed. The telephone rang twice and the girl's mother answered.

"I was expecting this call," the woman said. "My daughter told me everything. I've already notified my doctor."

Her rambling continued for at least five minutes. The silence was killing Rhonda. Shari just sat with the telephone to her ear, listening to the woman's every word. Finally, Shari got a few words in: "Is there anything we can do to help?"

Rhonda sighed. The tense look disappeared from her face. Her mind was at ease, but Rhonda continued to rock back and forth in her chair.

On the other end the of phone the woman replied, "Please don't be too hard on your son. He is a fine young man. My daughter said it was their first time and I believe her. Fifteen-year-olds today are not the same as when we were growing up. There is a lot of pressure out there."

"My son will go with you and your daughter to see the doctor," Shari said, still pretending to be Rhonda.

"That's a good idea," the woman said. "Let them both deal with reality head-on."

"He still hasn't said a word about this to me. I found out because I read a letter that he left in his pocket," Shari said. "I'll talk to him when he gets home. Thanks for being so understanding."

Shari hung up the telephone and hugged Rhonda.

"Were you crying because you thought his life would be messed up or because you didn't want to be a grandma at 39 years old?" Shari asked with a smirk on her face. "Tell the truth, girlfriend."

Rhonda laughed out loud and thanked Shari for taking charge. As for Shari's question about not wanting to be a young grandmother, Rhonda never did answer.

"That's okay—you don't have to answer me," Shari said. "But get prepared, because one day you will indeed be a grandmother, and from what I hear it's the best feeling in the world."

Been There, Done That

ELAINE WAS GLOWING. SHE HAD MET A NEW MAN AND PRACTI-cally overnight the quality of her life had improved 100 percent. No more Friday nights with her single girlfriends—she was busy with a new romance and couldn't have been happier.

"It's too good to be true," Elaine told her girlfriend, Gloria.

"Then you better beware," Gloria warned. "If you think it's too good to be true, it probably is—keep your guard up."

Elaine did the exact opposite. She had fallen head over heels in love with this man who sent her flowers, took her on romantic dates, and visited her regularly. There was just one problem—she never saw him on holidays.

"I bet he's married," Gloria told her friend. "Why else would he disappear for the holidays?"

"He's separated," Elaine argued. "In the process of getting a divorce, and he doesn't want to upset his children."

"Do you know for sure?" Gloria asked.

"Yes, he told me," she replied, getting a little annoyed.

"Well, do you have a home number for him?" Gloria asked.

"Yes. Now stop asking me all these questions," Elaine replied. "He's going to leave and we are going to live happily ever after. He just needs time to sort things out."

Gloria didn't want to be any more cynical than she had, but she didn't want Elaine to waste another minute with this guy. Gloria had been there, done that, and had her heart broken by a married man.

"Trust me on this one, honey," Gloria said, looking Elaine straight in the eye. "He will never leave his wife to be with you, and if he does, then he is not worth having because he will do the same to you one day."

Elaine continued making excuses for him, saying his wife was mean, evil, and unattractive. But Gloria knew there had to be another side to the story. "There always is," she told Elaine.

"I'm saying this because you're my friend and I want to be honest with you," Gloria said. "I honestly think you are kidding yourself to think this man will ever be yours. He'll keep stringing you on, if he can. Before you know it, you've invested a couple of years in a man who was never worth your time to begin with."

Gloria promised never to say another word about him after speaking her peace. Despite her friend's advice, Elaine continued to see him, and eventually he broke her heart—just like Gloria said he would. He did not get divorced, but instead he got his wife pregnant. Elaine saw them walking down the street hand in hand one day. Of course he tried to say it wasn't his baby when Elaine confronted him. She had pretended long enough that the relationship would work. Elaine finally realized he was never going to leave his wife.

Although embarrassed, Elaine knew she could call Gloria. Elaine was finally ready to be honest with her friend, and herself. As mad as she was at Gloria earlier, her friend was right and she owed Gloria an apology. It just goes to show you—sometimes our friends know us better than we know ourselves; they often see what we can't or don't want to see.

Pity Party

EVER HAVE ONE OF THOSE DAYS, WEEKS, OR EVEN MONTHS when it seems nothing is going right for you or any of your girlfriends? One girlfriend complains she is having a rough time at work; another friend is mad because her husband doesn't spend enough time with her and the kids. And if that's not enough, your best bud is freaking out because that hot and heavy date she had last week never called again. Not to mention you've got problems of your own, like the fact that your daughter flunked her chemistry exam and has to go to summer school.

Don't panic! Instead have a good old-fashioned pity party. That's right! Dust off some of those old blues albums (you know, the round pieces of plastic that used to play music before CDs came along), get your favorite munchies and drinks, and invite all those bummed-out girlfriends over to clear the air.

Once you've had time to relax, eat, drink, and catch up, get all the friends in a circle and take turns whining. Let each friend launch her complaint, then have all the others analyze it and help her solve it. The more friends at the pity party, the more fun and interesting it becomes. While there are a lot of women who like to keep personal problems close to the heart, you would be surprised to find out just how many other women have already been there, done that.

It's a wonderful girls' night out and it sure as hell beats

paying a therapist. Give it a shot and let your hair down. Create a safe spot and don't worry about anyone making fun of you—they wouldn't be there if they didn't need a little compassion, too. Guaranteed, by the end of the night everyone there will be laughing instead of crying the blues, 'cause you know you've got each other and hopefully have found a plan to make things better.

The Girlfriends' Network

ZENOBIA'S HUSBAND ERIC WAS A POPULAR NIGHTLY CABLE TV show host—a celebrity in his own right. The problem was he knew he was "special" and he took himself much too seriously. Zenobia's girlfriends adored her, but after a while they could not stand being around her husband, and it started affecting her friendships.

But when word spread that the network was revamping and Eric's contract would not be renewed, Zenobia panicked. She didn't know how their family would survive. They had saved some money, but not nearly enough to send their two teenage children to college. He interviewed with competitors, but they all wanted younger talent. Basically, there were no takers.

Over the next few months their nest egg dwindled. Eric couldn't find a job anywhere. Zenobia was scared to death and told her girlfriends she worried about paying the mortgage and feeding her kids. But one day, Sheila, one of Zenobia's friends, called out of the blue. She was the general manager of a start-up television network and offered Eric a job. He'd have to take a cut in pay and work longer hours, but out of desperation he decided to take it. He had to feed his family, after all. Zenobia was relieved and grateful to her friend.

When Eric showed up for work, Sheila, the kind friend who gave him the job, set the record straight.

"Let's get one thing straight," Sheila told him. "I didn't hire you based on your credentials or because you think you look good on television. I don't like your attitude and I expect you to check it at the door when you arrive each day. The *only* reason I hired you is because you are married to my girlfriend."

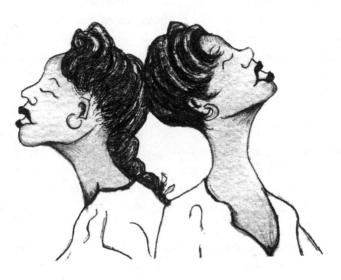

Actions Speak Louder

IT'S BEEN SAID THAT CHARITY BEGINS AT HOME, SO GIRLFRIENDS must do their share to help each other make it through the tough times. Whether your friend is down in the dumps because she's been laid off or she has suddenly gained weight, friends often need a little encouragement. When I asked women what they think the nicest thing is they've done to help a friend, here are some of the answers they came up with:

- Footed the bill for her to hire a housekeeper.
- Prepared a week's worth of food for her family after an operation.
- Babysat her kids while she went to the Bahamas.
- Treated her to theater tickets and dinner.
- Set her up on a blind date that ended up in marriage.
- Helped her move into her new apartment and painted it for her.
- Spent the night with her at the hospital when she was ill.
- Gave her a surprise party for her birthday.
- Sent her a plane ticket to visit.
- Stopped her from getting drunk at a party.
- Cosigned for her to buy a car.
- Punched her ex-boyfriend in the face for putting her down.
- Wrote her research paper so that she could graduate high school.

- Helped her start an exercise routine.
- Left work early to comfort her after a fight with her man.
- Anonymously deposited $500 into her checking account.
- Took her on a shopping spree.
- Double dated with a guy I hated because her date was fine.
- Stood by her side in the delivery room.
- Helped her lie on her U.S. Customs declaration form.
- Comforted her after she tested HIV positive.
- Drove her across country and back.
- Helped her escape from an abusive husband.
- Ordered her a credit card, under my own line of credit.
- Went with her fiancé to pick out an engagement ring she'd love.
- Treated her to a massage and makeover.
- Took her to church and introduced her to God.

At a Loss

REGINA HAD ALWAYS BEEN A LOOKER. TALL, THIN, AND shapely with a beautiful smile. So when her husband died unexpectedly of a heart attack, it was no surprise that the single men in the town started calling and inviting her out.

"I have this great guy for you." "Would you like to go to a movie?" "You must be lonely. I would like to take you to dinner." She heard these things over and over. Within four months of her husband's death, she thought she had heard every cheap pickup line. She was desperately lonely and all she wanted was her husband back. He had been her best friend for years and she missed the love, laughter, and companionship they shared.

When she was feeling really low, she received a phone call from her husband's college buddy, Jim. He had no idea his fraternity brother had passed on and Regina had to break the news. Jim was in town for business and insisted that Regina have dinner with him and his new bride. She reluctantly agreed to meet Jim and Kitty at a nearby restaurant.

When she arrived, Jim and Kitty were at a table with a bouquet of flowers for Regina.

"It's so good to see you," Jim said. "This is my wife, Kitty."

"Pleased to meet you," Kitty said.

"You too," Regina replied. "Larry's death happened so suddenly. I didn't have time to notify everyone."

"I understand, Regina," Jim said. And she suddenly felt oddly comfortable.

They chatted, laughed, and shared fond stories about Larry. For the first time in months, she saw a glimpse of happiness. Jim and Kitty seemed to know all the right things to say.

"Too bad you don't live here," Regina said.

"Be careful what you wish for," Jim joked. "We just may end up being your neighbor, if this business deal works out the way I plan."

"Really?" Regina replied. "What's going on?"

"Well, I'll tell you in a minute, but first will you ladies excuse me a moment."

Jim went to the men's room and the women had a chance for a little girl talk.

"So how long have you and Jim been married?" Regina asked.

"A little over three months," Kitty replied.

"And how did you meet?" Regina prodded playfully.

"Through a mutual friend," Kitty said. "Actually, I was a widow, too. My first husband died of cancer and I didn't think anyone else could ever make me happy again. And then came Jim."

"That's wonderful," Regina said. "I've been invited out a lot since Larry died, but I can't bring myself to go. It's much too soon."

"I thought the same thing," Kitty said. "Give it time. Things will change. My children, relatives, and friends came over regularly right after my Herbie died and then it stopped. My dearest friend and her husband were the only ones who came on a regular basis. One night they brought Jim and we've been together ever since. Nobody will ever replace Herbie or Larry, but life must move forward. If we are lucky enough to find another companion, then we should consider ourselves blessed."

"But Larry and I had been happily married 26 years," Regina said, shaking her head with disbelief. "And there was still so much we wanted to do."

Regina started crying and Kitty embraced her as if they'd been friends all their lives. Just then Jim returned to see the women embracing. Regina and Kitty bonded. It didn't take long.

The night ended on a very bright note. Regina hadn't felt this good since Larry died.

The next morning, Regina's telephone rang. It was Kitty. The deal went through and they were relocating to Charlotte.

"This is wonderful," Regina said. "I had such a good time last night. I knew in my heart everything would work out."

"Me too," Kitty said. "And I'm going to have to start house hunting. Do you know any realtors?"

"I know them all," Regina said. "There are several developments out here in Davis Lake, where I live. I'm talking beautiful, girl."

"Okay, give me a call in Atlanta and let me know when I can come back," Kitty said. "Gotta go. Just wanted you to be the first to know. And Regina? Don't forget what I said. Nobody can replace Larry, but life doesn't stop here for you. I know you will find happiness again."

"I already have," Regina said. "I found it in you."

Saving for a Rainy Day

MAGGIE'S HUSBAND HAD ALWAYS GIVEN HER THE BEST OF everything. A custom-built five-bedroom house with a perfectly manicured lawn. A nanny, housekeeper, diamonds, furs, romantic vacations—you name it! Benny adored Maggie and showered her with his affection and gifts.

You see, Benny was an old-fashioned guy who believed it was his job to bring home the bacon. In turn, he also expected Maggie to stay home and be a mother to their twin daughters.

Benny never told Maggie how much money his two liquor stores brought in and she never asked. All Maggie knew was that they were comfortable. But one day, 15 years into their marriage, all that changed! Benny walked into the house, head hung low, with tears in his eyes.

"We need to talk," he said, cutting straight to the chase. "I've put this off long enough. We are in serious financial trouble."

"What?" Maggie laughed with disbelief.

"It's true, I make a decent amount of money from the liquor stores," Benny confessed. "I had also been doing very well with the stock market. As fast as I made money, I spent it. Now I've blown it all."

Maggie was in shock. She blamed herself for leaving her $35,000-a-year teaching job after she gave birth to the twins. She never questioned their financial situation because she had no reason to. Now she regretted it.

"I'm so sorry, baby," Benny said. "We are three months behind on the mortgage. Two months behind on the car payments. And two of my credit cards are maxed out. I've already called about getting a second mortgage, but I am waiting to hear back."

Instead of crying or getting mad, Maggie got busy. They went through all their bills and monthly expenses, and figured out how they could cut back. They decided the live-in housekeeper would be the first to go. Benny sold his sailboat and Maggie sold a few pieces of jewelry. That gave them a couple thousand dollars but not enough to wipe out their debt.

The next day, Benny went to work and Maggie secretly went to the bank. She had never told Benny, but years ago before she and Benny were married she set up a separate checking account. That evening, when Benny walked in the door, she had a candlelight gourmet dinner on the table, complete with champagne, a waiter, and Maggie's best friend Patti.

"Have you lost your mind?" Benny asked, alarmed.

"No, I haven't," Maggie replied calmly.

"Then why would you go all out like this, knowing we are in serious financial trouble?" Benny asked.

"We *were* in trouble," Maggie said. "Truth of the matter is that I've always had a separate checking account in addition to our joint account. Most women do. When we got married, 15 years ago, Patti forced me to keep my account. A nest egg, just in case we ever had a rainy day."

Maggie handed over a check for $43,000. Benny let out a sigh of relief and then hugged Maggie and Patti at the same time. "So you two stay-at-home moms have been doing more than just baking cookies over the years?"

"Yes, we have," Patti said. "We've been preparing for a rainy day."

"Thank you, baby," Benny said, tears in his eyes.

"Don't thank me, thank Patti," Maggie said. "Without our friend Patti, we'd be in big trouble. Please take her advice and get a financial planner so this never happens again."

"Definitely. You got it ladies," Benny responded. "Here's to my two favorite girls."

And with that the three friends sat down to a delicious candlelight dinner. Patti and Maggie grinned and winked at each other all night. Just between girlfriends, they knew the account was not closed out. Maggie continued to keep her secret account.

Betrayed by a Friend

$\mathcal{J}$OYCE BECAME AN OLD LADY BEFORE HER TIME, COMPLAINing of arthritis, bad knees, and hot flashes the day she turned 45. Her neighbor and girlfriend, Ceil, warned Joyce that being a homebody would jeopardize her marriage to Brad, who still enjoyed an active life.

"Then you go with him to the dinner-dance," Joyce told her. "That way, you'll have an escort and Brad will have to be on his best behavior."

Neither Ceil nor Brad felt comfortable with the arrangement at first, but Joyce insisted. At the dance everyone asked where Joyce was.

"Not feeling well," Brad answered.

"So she suggested that I keep an eye on Brad," Ceil chimed in.

Soon one escort became two. Joyce never wanted to go out, so she kept sending her girlfriend to take care of Brad. After Ceil and Brad attended a few dances together, rumors began to swirl. Everyone knew that Joyce was not a social butterfly, but they couldn't understand why she let Ceil be her constant stand-in. Brad had a reputation for being a ladies' man. Though Brad and Ceil denied the rumors of a love affair, eventually they found themselves in an awkward position. What started out as one innocent night turned into a peck on the cheek the next night, a passionate kiss the next date, and eventually a steamy full-fledged affair.

In the meantime, Joyce was oblivious and became more involved with church, which frowned upon drinking and partying. Before long her 20-year marriage began to crumble, and guess who was there to pick up the pieces? Ceil.

But what Joyce didn't know was that her girlfriend had fallen in love with her husband. They hid their affection in public, but behind closed doors they were quite intimate. Eventually, Joyce grew suspicious. Ceil made herself more and more scarce. She seldom returned Joyce's phone calls, and when she did the conversation was short and cold. Instead, Ceil continued to spend time with Brad.

At the urging of another girlfriend, Joyce paid Ceil an unexpected visit. When Ceil opened the door, Brad was sitting on her couch, shirtless with his feet nestled in a pair of slippers. Framed photographs of Ceil and Brad were scattered around the living room. There was no doubt these two were having an affair. Joyce remained calm; she believed a higher power was guiding her. It had to be.

"Please excuse us, Brad," Joyce said in a voice a little louder than a whisper. "Ceil and I need to talk. I will speak to you at home."

Brad tried to explain, but Joyce simply pointed to the door. Ceil immediately began to cry. She had taken her girlfriend for granted and betrayed her trust, and now she had to face her.

"Had I not developed a close relationship with the Lord, I would not be this calm," Joyce said, her voice still soft and angelic. "I would've probably walked in here cussin' you out and ready to fight. Instead, I want you to know that I am not surprised, at least not by Brad's behavior. We've been down this road before—his secretary, some woman on his bowling team, and God only knows who else. But *you?* How could you of all people fall for his game? You wiped my tears after every affair. You convinced me to forgive him, for the children's sake, though you knew my heart ached. Brad will always disappoint me, but I never expected this from you. You are my friend."

Ceil tried to get a word in, but Joyce quickly silenced her.

"Shhhhh," Joyce said, placing her right index finger over her mouth. "Your actions have already spoken for you. Now, it's my turn to talk. My marriage to Brad was over the first time he cheated, but for our kids we will continue to live as husband and wife. When it comes to him, well, I can not miss something or someone I never had. But you, Ceil, I will miss you desperately because I truly believed you were my friend. It's too bad you let your lonely heart choose to have a fling with Brad, instead of allowing your loving heart to remain a faithful friend. Maybe someday I will be able to forgive you, but for now I will go on as if you've gone away—far away."

Pleasant Surprise

Daisy and Wayne had been married just over two years when they stumbled upon Wayne's old college sweetheart, Sarena, and her fiancé at a party. Though everyone feared it would be awkward, as soon as Wayne introduced the women they immediately hit it off. Within minutes, they realized they had much more in common than just Wayne. Daisy was an insurance agent and Sarena was a realtor working in the same city. They were both smart and ambitious and members of the same sorority. In the short time they spent together, they came up with all kinds of ideas to network and collaborate on business ventures. They immediately exchanged cards and promised to stay in touch.

A few days later, Daisy called Sarena to set up a lunchtime business meeting. They planned to talk business, but instead ended up at Macy's one-day sale. They spent hours trying on dresses, shoes, and anything and everything that was on sale.

"That looks good on you, girl," Sarena said about an animal-print mini-skirt.

"Sold!" Daisy replied, adding another dress to her pile of keepers.

Somewhere between the designer dress racks and shoe department, a friendship was about to blossom. Though it was Wayne who essentially brought them together, it was their brains, personality, and love of shopping that became the basis of their friendship. In fact, Wayne started to feel like the odd man out and felt a twinge of jealousy that his wife seemed to have more fun with his ex-girlfriend than him. But he quickly got over it—he had no choice since the girls were practically inseparable.

Now shopping has become Daisy and Sarena's Saturday morning ritual, along with a strong cup of coffee and a stack of banana pancakes. Occasionally, they discuss business, but for the most part they just have fun. One Saturday morning, Daisy confessed: "You have a beautiful spirit. I know why you and Wayne were college sweethearts. I'm glad he always had good taste in women."

And Wayne too came to love their friendship. In fact, he gets a kick out of Daisy as his wife and Sarena as his "girl-friend." It just goes to show you—sometimes friendships form and blossom under the most unlikely circumstances. Hey, you never know!

Girlfriends' Getaway Guide

Just Between Girlfriends
Social Calendar

Wʜᴇɴ ᴡᴀꜱ ᴛʜᴇ ʟᴀꜱᴛ ᴛɪᴍᴇ ʏᴏᴜ ꜱᴘᴇɴᴛ ꜱᴏᴍᴇ ᴛɪᴍᴇ ᴡɪᴛʜ ʏᴏᴜʀ girlfriends? Not at a kiddie party (where you asked your girlfriend to put on the Big Bird costume to entertain the kids), softball game, or the church picnic. I'm talking about a girls' night out. Well, if you haven't done it in a while, pull out your calendar and your telephone book. Call up your girlfriends and start making plans to have a little fun.

You see, when friendships last through seasons you definitely have more than a reason to celebrate. No need to call on Martha Stewart for ideas. My friends say I have just the creativity to be Martha's heir apparent. I've come up with a Just Between Girlfriends month-to-month calendar of events that is sure to keep you and your girlfriends busy and well entertained. Whether it's something as simple as a Valentine's Day grab bag surprise or a backyard fashion show featuring your Mother's Day outfit—each event is designed to get your girlfriends together for some good old-fashioned fun.

These monthly activities can be tailored for as many or as few girlfriends as you'd like to include. And there's no reason why you can't pick and choose which activities best suit your lifestyle. The whole idea of each activity is to secure the ties that bind and celebrate the uniqueness of our girlfriends. While I know not everyone feels comfortable hosting parties, brunches, or gatherings, I've included some user-friendly tips and a section on suggested menus to make every event a guaranteed success. Look out, Martha!

January: Just Between Girlfriends
New Year's Day Brunch

Whether you had a date to bring in the New Year or not, gather your girlfriends for a Just Between Girlfriends New Year's Day Brunch. Tell your husband, boyfriend, or your baby's daddy that before he watches college football bowl games he'll have to watch the kid(s). You have a date with your girlfriends. Assign a hostess or two who will be responsible for setting the time, place, and budget for the brunch. If you decide to have it in a restaurant, make reservations early, but I think gatherings at someone's home are more intimate and personal. If you do it at someone's home, ask each friend to bring a dish (see the "Menus and Ideas" section). Better yet, if you are in a pinch for time, chip in for a caterer, who will cook and clean.

Once all your friends are together, hand out a piece of paper, preferably with a beautiful color scheme or design, and have them write down three New Year's resolutions. Remind them to be realistic. On the back side of the paper, also have them write three goals they want to achieve in the New Year. Make sure their name is not on the list. Put the pieces of paper in a decorative shopping bag. As you and your friends enjoy brunch, each person will pick a list from the bag, read it, and try to guess which friend wrote it. After the friend's identity is known, discuss solutions and ways to help your friend reach her goal. Then make a date to get together a month or two from now to see how those resolutions are coming. What the heck—it's another excuse to get the girls together once again. You are sure to wish this party never ends.

February: Valentine's Day Friendship Grab Bag

Okay, not everyone has a sweetheart or hubby, but we do all have girlfriends. So instead of waiting for Mr. Right or Mr. Right-Now to make your day, show some love for a special girlfriend. If you have a group of friends who need a little extra love on this day (like the unofficial single mommy club that some of my friends and I have seemed to form) make a pact to exchange Valentine's Day surprises. Don't try to send a dozen roses or a box of chocolates. Be creative. A little thought goes a long way. For example, in honor of Black History Month, which also falls in February, shower your friend with a gift that has an Afrocentric flair.

Instead of sending red roses to her job, send an African violet or tickets for an African-American exhibit or play. And if soul food is what she likes, but she shies away from it because of all the calories, splurge and take her out for soul food at her favorite spot. If your friend loves to read, get her an autographed book signed by her favorite author. For the music lover, buy her a new CD, or better yet, make a tape of her favorite love songs. And if your girlfriend collects dolls, crystals, or even snow globes (like me, *hint, hint*), add something to her collection. There are a million things friends can do to celebrate their love for each other. A gift from the heart is everlasting, especially when your girlfriend is not expecting it.

March: Girlfriends' Spring Cleaning

Designate one Saturday during early spring to be the official Girlfriends' Spring Cleaning Day. I'm not talking about waxing floors or cleaning windows—that's between your girlfriend and her housekeeper. I *am* talking about something fun, like helping her clean out her closet. If we all look deep within the walls of our closets we'll probably find our high school prom dress, a pair of Gloria Vanderbilt jeans, or possibly an old bell-bottom pantsuit that has come back in style, but unfortunately it's too snug. Don't waste another minute—get rid of it, girlfriend.

Have your friend pull the oldies and have her tell you about how she was the talk of the party when she wore that sequined baseball jacket with the matching hat (every outfit has a story). Linda and I not only know the story of each outfit already, we were probably together the day the item was purchased. When your friend is finished bragging or perhaps complaining that she should have worn a different color shoe, tell her to toss it. If she can't seem to part with it, take a Polaroid of her in it (or trying to squeeze in it) for the last time—put it in a box and donate the items to a local church , charity, or relative.

While everything may not be too small or too outdated, the truth of the matter is that most of us have more clothes than we really need, and you can help someone by bundling up a few items and making a clothing donation. The pictures you snap of your friend in the clothes can be arranged in an album that will become a lasting keepsake. And I can tell you now that you and your friends will have a lot of laughs along the way.

April: The Girlfriends' Shower

You don't need a girlfriend with an engagement ring on her finger or a big belly to have a shower—celebrate the strength and beauty of your girlfriends with a special shower in their honor. The sisterhood of friendship is a unique union that helps enhance the quality of our life. We call on our girlfriends to find a good babysitter, dentist, or plumber. They are there as we celebrate milestones such as our 16th, 21st, 30th, 45th, and 60th birthdays, as well as our silver and gold wedding anniversaries. And when we are emotionally drained or frustrated, our girlfriends are by our side to offer a little relief. So why not have a shower to show a little appreciation.

Set a date and then send out invitations, as if it were a baby or bridal shower. Decorate the room with lots of pretty balloons and flowers, serve finger foods, and pop open a couple of bottles of Moët to mark the day. Play shower games and hand out small prizes to the winners. For an added treat, hire a singer, comedian, magician, manicurist, or invite a local author to read from his/her latest book.

When you say good-bye to your friends, do it in style—present them with a small favor or goody bag so that they will always remember the day. Your girlfriends will love and appreciate this unexpected gesture.

May: Mother's Day Fashion Show

Whether you are a mother or not, gather up your girlfriends, their moms, mother-in-laws, aunties, godmothers, and whoever else wants to have a little fun after church on Mother's Day. Either reserve the church's fellowship hall, a community recreation center, or set up a makeshift runway in your backyard for women of all ages to strut their stuff at the Mother's Day Fashion Show. Let your girlfriend with the biggest mouth and most outgoing personality serve as the mistress of ceremonies, describing each woman's outfit from hat to shoes. Bring out the CD player, which will give the Mother's Day models a chance to really work it, and get the rest of the crowd cheering and whistling.

Have a friend who takes the best pictures (in my circle, that's definitely Shelley and Natalie) photograph each mom. And have the kids, husbands, and boyfriends serve cookies and punch to your guests. The fashion show can be as long or short as you'd like. The main purpose is to have fun and pay tribute to all the mothers who work so hard all year keeping their family together. It's a great way for moms to feel beautiful and special for the day. Sit back and enjoy being queen for a day.

June: Adopt a Bride

June is a big wedding month, so why not add a littler cheer to someone's life by helping with wedding plans. Find a friend, relative, or member of your church who's getting married and offer to help do something special for her. It can be a close friend, or an acquaintance, but the gesture will be appreciated. If you are good at applying makeup, styling hair, or decorating, offer to help her the day before the wedding, or on the big day itself. Or perhaps you could help the blushing bride-to-be design her ceremony programs on your home computer or help organize her seating chart. If you know of a bride who is short on cash, have a bake sale and give the donations to the bride for her gown, shoes, or even a honeymoon. But whatever you do, work within her plans, make suggestions based only on your area of expertise, and let her have the final say.

With my busy schedule, I declined to be the mistress of ceremony for my girlfriend Denene's wedding, but I volunteered to set up her honeymoon suite. At her reception, she slipped me the keys and my date and I went to her hotel room and prepared it for the bride and groom. We sprinkled rose petals up the spiral staircase, arranged several dozen candles throughout the bedroom and bathroom, filled her bathtub with all kinds of sweet-smelling goodies, and dropped Godiva chocolate all over the room. We also filled the bride's special request that included champagne, whipped cream, and strawberries. Denene called the room from the limo and we began lighting the candles. We snuck out before the newlyweds walked in. They later told me they were delighted.

No matter what you decide to do, every bride needs a good friend to help her organize her special day. So get caught up in the love and happiness of someone's special day. Your kindness will be remembered forever.

July: Christmas in July Barbecue

Your friends are sure to scratch their heads in disbelief, but I guarantee they will be at your house to celebrate Christmas in July. Set up the artificial tree, complete with garland, lights, and ornaments. That's right—go all out, catch some of the off-season sales, and stock up on Christmas goodies. Ask each friend to bring an unwrapped toy or book that will be donated to a family or charity of your choice. There are lots of children out there whose parents are barely making ends meet or are dealing with a crisis. Bring a little sunshine into their life by distributing the toys you've collected for them.

Dust off the Christmas CDs and tapes and play only holiday music at the party. Sure, your neighbors might think you've lost it, but your guests will be in a yuletide state of mind. A visit from Santa would also be fun. He can lead your

This is a nice way to bring a busy summer to a close. You'll probably be spending the next week or so getting the children ready for school, or dreading the fact that your workload is about to increase, so why not have one last summer fling with those you love—your girlfriends!

September: African-American Beauties

Look out Miss America, let the chocolate beauties have their moment in the spotlight. There will be no competition for these girlfriends, only a day of pampering at a spa. That's right, a day of beauty. Wake up early in the morning and meet for coffee and a bagel. Then hit the mall to get a dress for tonight, when you and your girlfriends will get all dolled up and go out on the town. If your girlfriends want to invite their man, let them; if they want to go solo, that's cool, too.

Check into the spa (or treat yourself to a new hairdo, pedicure, and manicure). If you have the nerve, dip into an upscale department store and let one of the professionals at the makeup counter give you a new look. Interface Cosmetics is a sistah-friendly company with great shades for African-American beauties. Get a massage, mud mask, and sauna, and take before, during, and after pictures so that you can see just how much or little work it took to make you beautiful. Hire a limo to drive you and your girlfriends to the restaurant. After dinner, take in a jazz show or go dancing at

guests in a few rounds of "Santa Says" or maybe even
electric slide. Who knows, Santa just might end up bein
male dancer. And after the sun goes down, plug in yc
Christmas tree. Have a seasonal sing-along and share chil
hood Christmas memories, like how you always managed t
find the toys before Santa left them under the tree. Believe
me, everyone will leave the party in great spirits, and just
think of how happy you will make those kids who are getting
a brightly wrapped present for no reason at all.

August: Back to the Beach Party

So what if you can't fit into that slinky little black bikini anymore—that's no reason to avoid the beach. There are all
kinds of flattering bathing suits for us voluptuous women,
and if you still don't feel comfortable get a cover-up or
sarong—and get over it! A day at the beach is all about having fun, so round up your girlfriends and head for the beach
like you used to when you were a young girl.

Pack a lunch, lots of beverages, a beach ball, a camera,
your kid's boom box, and don't forget the binoculars. Just because you're married doesn't mean you can't look. Build a
sand castle or bury your friends in the sand. Play a round of
"Truth, Dare, Consequences," using unsuspecting beachgo-
ers as the object of each challenge. When the excitement of
enjoying a day at the beach without the kids wears off, form
a circle and take turns reading your favorite poem, short
story, or passage from a novel to your friends.

your favorite spot. Girlfriends should help each other to pamper themselves and to keep themselves feeling beautiful. It doesn't hurt to keep your girlfriends' romances alive or help those single ladies find a man of their own.

October: Girlfriends' Getaway Weekend

You survived this year's family vacation and the kids are settled into their school routine. Now, you deserve a little break to unwind and reflect on yet another year. Call up your girlfriends near and far and decide where you'll meet for an upcoming three-day weekend. Perhaps the Bahamas, Grand Cayman, or a resort that's not too far from home. Just you and the girls, taking a trip to sun and fun.

If your budget doesn't allow you to splurge to that degree, pool your money and check in to a hotel suite in an undisclosed location not far from home. Leave a beeper number where the family can reach you, but only in the event of an emergency. As a group, visit a tourist attraction that you've always wanted to see but never had the time. Take in a movie or get tickets to a sporting event. Be sure to take a dip in the hotel pool and have a drink in the lobby bar. Then treat yourself to breakfast in bed and allow yourself the flexibility to catch up on your sleep.

Regardless of where you go, just make sure you and your girlfriends get away, even if you camp out at a friend's house for the weekend—at least you can enjoy a little downtime.

November: Pin the Tail on the Turkey

With Thanksgiving quickly approaching and family gatherings being planned, reserve an evening to play "Pin the Tail
on the Turkey" and have some fun. Though we know turkeys
don't really have tails, I've come up with a silly little game
with the sole purpose of making you laugh. So look through
your photo albums for a picture of an ex-husband, old
boyfriend, selfish lover, fake friend, mean mother-in-law,
ruthless boss, or anyone who has done you wrong in the past.
After all these years, your girlfriends are finally going to help
you get the closure you've always searched for. Enlarge the
pictures and bring the blowups to the party.

Have each girlfriend tape the picture of her jive turkey to
the wall. As she is hanging his/her mug shot, she will have 5
to 10 minutes (depending on how many friends are playing)
to tell the horrible story of her turkey. Once she's finished, her
friends will write down comments about the turkey on a
piece of paper cut out in the shape of a tail. The friends will
blindfold the turkey owner and she will try to pin the tails on
the turkey. The blindfold is then removed and she reads each
comment out loud. For an added treat, see if she can guess
who wrote each comment. Though some of the stories may
be heartwrenching, the comments should provide a little
comic relief. You're sure to find out something new about
your girlfriends this night! Throw in prizes for extra silly
comments. Have fun!

December: Holiday Cookie Swap

Doesn't it seem that your girlfriends always have the best holiday cookies? I know my girlfriend Karen Lombardi's cookies are always delicious. Her cookies are perfect in shape, size, and taste. Your girlfriend swears her recipe has been passed down from generation to generation, though you think Mrs. Fields may have given her a hand in the kitchen. Put her to the ultimate test—invite her to participate in a holiday cookie swap, which is an idea borrowed from my girlfriend Rahda. With Christmas and Kwanzaa sneaking up on you, there's no way you'll have time to do a variety of holiday baking. Instead, invite five friends to bake six dozen of their favorite cookies (the object is to get a variety) and the hostess will bake six dozen of her favorite cookies, too.

Set a date, then host a coffee klatch to swap cookies and recipes. There's always one friend who puts too many nuts in her chocolate chip cookies or someone who ends up buying her cookies from a bakery, but the stories friends share over holiday cookies and coffee are usually from the heart.

And don't forget to bring a big cookie jar or tray to take your six dozen cookies home. Whether baked in your oven or the oven at your local grocery store, at least you made a sincere effort to spend a little time with your girlfriends over the holidays.

Late December: New Year's Eve Gong Show

Time is running out. Still don't have a date to bring in the New Year? That's okay. I bet a lot of your girlfriends don't, either. So rather than panic about scrounging up a date for the night, spend it with people you really know, love, and trust— your girlfriends. If you don't feel like going out on the town, here's a fun suggestion. Make plans to attend a church service with your friends (while you are there, pray for a date next year) and then celebrate the New Year with an old-fashioned gong show—that's sure to start the year off with a bang (or a gong depending on your talent). Chances are, you don't have a gong, but you do have a cabinet full of pots and pans. Set up the biggest ones you have on a table and tell your friends to bring a wooden spoon to the party. Then throw a tape in the video camera, set it up on the tripod, and start the show. It will definitely be hilarious; I'd be willing to put money on that.

Take turns performing. If your friend does well, then applaud her; if she doesn't, gong her. After the gong, do the famous dance that Gene-Gene the Dancing Machine used to do to on the old TV show. If you don't know it, ask someone to show you. Trust me, this will become very amusing and friends will want a copy of the tape to save for days when they are feeling a little down. And when the gong show is over and your belly hurts from laughing, don't forget to break out the champagne. Toast to good times, a new year, and most important of all, good friends!

Menus & Ideas

Just Between Girlfriends
New Year's Day Brunch

Menu #1
Fruit Salad or Fresh Fruit
Black-Eyed Pea Soup
Crispy Baked Chicken
Rice & Gravy
Cinnamon & Honey-glazed Carrots
Fresh String Beans
Homemade Bread
Champagne Punch
Coconut Custard Pie
Coffee

Menu #2
Banana-Pecan Waffles
Spicy Fried Chicken
Scrambled Cheddar Eggs
Hot Cider

Menu #3
Golden Brown Fried Catfish
Home Fries
Coleslaw
Buttery Biscuits
Mimosas

Suggestions

Invitations: Get a package of decorative paper with the matching envelopes and whip up an invitation on your home computer. Make it elegant, but keep it simple. Sprinkle a little confetti into the envelope or some perfume-scented rose petals to add a nice touch. Mail two weeks in advance.

Setting the Table: Go ahead and pull out your fine china. That's right, girlfriend—you know it's been in the curio or packed away since you hosted Christmas dinner four years ago. If you are like me, single, and without china, then use the "good plates" or good-quality paper plates. Whatever you decide, make sure all the plates, flatware, and glasses match. If you don't have a tablecloth, a solid-colored sheet can double for a tablecloth. Sprinkle the same confetti or rose petals on the table as you sprinkled in the envelope. If you don't have a silk floral arrangement around the house to use for a centerpiece, then pull one of those gifts from under the tree that hasn't made it to its owner. Put the box or boxes on the table, flanked by two candles or two bottles of champagne. Dress up the bottles or candles by tying ribbon (the same color as confetti) around them.

Food: Set it up on the kitchen counter or on another table. Presentation is everything, so be creative. Don't serve out of pots. Let your friends feel special. If you want to add an extra flair, release helium balloons throughout the dining room.

Music: Play some of that good old-fashioned sing-along music such as Aretha Franklin's double CD, or anything by Stevie Wonder, Marvin Gaye, or Gladys Knight. Gospel music is also a winner (especially Yolanda Adams), or ask each guest to bring their favorite CD.

Favors: I always like to send my friends home with a little something to remember the day. Here are some ideas: a journal so that they can write about the day, or a picture frame. If you give the frame, remember to take pictures. If those items are too pricey because you have more than 10 guests, go to a discount store and buy acrylic frames. Sometimes you can luck out and get two for a dollar. Then get an opaque paint marker that will permanently cover nearly any surface and write a special message or the date. If you want to add a little more pizzazz, use the same kind of confetti or rose petals you used for the table, lace, African print fabric, or tiny decorative ornaments and glue in the corners of the frame.

An alternative for the journal is to buy a small notebook for each friend and decorate it with fabric, contact paper, wrapping paper, or even newspaper.

Valentine's Day Grab-Bag

Suggestions

Chances are that you and your girlfriends had so much fun at last month's brunch that you'll want to get together again. Valentine's Day is the perfect time to celebrate the love you have for your girlfriends. A week before Valentine's Day, pick names for the grab bag or decide that each gift will be given randomly.

Set a Gift Price: Set a universal price limit between $10 and $100 so that nobody feels cheated.

Gift Ideas: Be creative. Think about what she would like, not you. Every year my girlfriend Shelley gives me a photo album filled with all the newspaper articles I've written all year. She takes a simple album and decorates it. On the inside cover she writes me a special note. I look forward to Shelley's gift because I don't always have time to clip. Think about her hobbies, career, and interests.

Venue: Meet as a group the day before Valentine's Day or the holiday itself if it fits into everyone's schedule. Reserve a table at your favorite restaurant, bookstore cafe, or coffee shop. Have an open discussion about your best and worst Valentine's Day and then exchange gifts. If you are single, let your friends know you are actively looking for a mate and ask for their help.

Extra: Keep in mind that February is also Black History Month, so try to drop some knowledge about our people and our struggle on your girlfriends, too. Talk about the love you have for one of your relatives who has passed on, or our ancestors, such as Ida B. Wells, Sojourner Truth, or Rosa Parks. You can also read your favorite poem and hand out copies to your friends. My favorite poem is Maya Angelou's "Phenomenal Woman." I get chills every time I read it out loud.

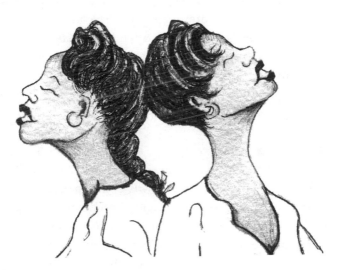

Girlfriends' Spring Cleaning

Suggestions

When you arrive at your girlfriend's house be sure to have a positive attitude. This activity may be extremely emotional. But be prepared to give her the comfort she needs in order to get rid of the clothes.

Things to Do: Encourage your girlfriend to talk about what role the outfit played in her life. When I help Linda clean her giant walk-in closet, there is one outfit that's sure to make us laugh. We got all dolled up one night (she had on a black silk mini-skirt suit and I wore a pair of black spandex biker shorts with an eggshell blazer) to attend a star-studded premiere of one of Spike Lee's movies. We were looking good. On our way to the party, it just poured and there was nowhere to hide. We were drenched. All we could do was laugh, go home, and watch the party on the news.

What to Bring: A box of tissues to wipe your girlfriend's tears. The thought of throwing away clothes may result in tears. A cup of her favorite coffee will also help ease the tension. Bring a camera so you can capture each outfit your girlfriend slips into on film. Try to remember her comments and write captions for each picture when they are arranged in a photo album. When you decorate the photo album, be sure to put a flattering picture on the cover. You want her to be pleased to receive it.

Charity: Just in case your friend hasn't called charities to donate her clothes, be sure to do a little research yourself. Identifying three charities or people in need will give your girlfriend a chance to choose. If you two really want something to do, sell all the clothes in a garage sale and donate the proceeds to your favorite charity. Make sure you get a letter of receipt so that you can claim the donation on your taxes.

Ditto: Set a date for her to return the favor.

The Girlfriends' Shower

Menu #1
Buffalo Chicken Wings
Barbecued Wings
Sweet & Sour Wings
Pasta Salad
Chopped Salad
Dinner Rolls
Carrot Cake
Rum Punch

Menu #2
Barbecued Shrimp
Fried Chicken Strips
Baked Ziti
Steamed Veggies
Miniature Club Rolls
Coconut Pineapple Layer Cake
Iced Coffee

Menu #3

Sliced Filet Mignon
Sliced Roast Turkey Breast
Rice & Red Beans
Shredded Lettuce & Carrots with Ginger Sauce
Sliced Tomatoes
Toasted Pita Squares
Banana Puddin' Pie
Pineapple/Banana Colada

Suggestions

Invitations: Be bold! Be daring! Create excitement. The invitation is like a sneak peek of the party. Design or buy invitations that reflect your personality and/or desire to make your girlfriends feel special. Send invitations via a message in a bottle, a cassette, or videotape, drop them in a box, and wrap them, fax them, or place an ad in the classifieds. Mail at least two weeks in advance.

Decorations: Make sure your decorations carry the theme, design, color, or motif of the shower. Don't send glittery gold or silver invites and have red, black, and green decorations—that's a big no-no! Be consistent. Fresh flowers, helium balloons, and streamers always work nicely. And scatter disposable cameras around the room.

Entertainment: If you know a youngster who sings, recites poetry, or tells a good joke, invite her/him to come and perform. Hire a manicurist or magician. Call the local book editor to try to find an author to read from her latest book. Tell all the guests to bring their high school yearbook or a photo album if you want to keep the entertainment just between girlfriends.

Shower Games: Take a passage from a romance novel, deleting names, places, and other particulars. Have each guest fill in the blanks, substituting their words for what's in the passage. Play the old childhood game, Telephone. Limbo. Simon Says. Soul Train Line. Charades based on situations that involve friends. Unscramble letters into familiar words. Girlfriends' Jeopardy.

Favors: A magnet. Scarf. Shower gel. Soaps. Book of poetry. Personalized T-shirts and caps. Pins. Costume jewelry. Movie ticket. Flavored coffee. Notecards. Make sure each favor is the same and wrapped beautifully.

Goody Bags: Filled with girly stuff, like tissues, gum, tampons, candy, aspirin, travel-size goods, pen, coupons, nuts, wine, knee-hi's, rain bonnet, sewing kit, perfume samples, puzzle books, planner.

Mother's Day Fashion Show

Menu #1
Grilled Chicken Nachos
Mother's Day Sheet Cake
Peach Iced Tea

Menu #2
Cheese & Crackers
Fresh Veggies
Onion Dip
Oatmeal Raisin Cookies
Cranberry-Orange Punch

Menu #3
Beef & Chicken Tacos
Fruit Platter
Pecan Chocolate Chip Cookies
Root Beer Float

Suggestions

Props: Make a runway out of large pieces of wood. Cover it with pieces of leftover carpet. Use a plastic runner. If you have a patio, let that serve as the stage or raised runway. Make sure heels will not sink into dirt. Set up chairs in a semicircle.

Music: Bring your kids' boom box outside or simply raise the window and set the speaker outside. Make sure all the music is lively and upbeat, like "No Diggity," "Hey Mr. DJ," "I'm Every Woman," "Stomp," "Ain't No Stoppin' Us Now," "Second Time Around," "Shoop," "Keep Your Head Up."

Favors: Give the mothers a keepsake to mark this special day. A bookmark, photo key chain, an assortment of teas, ice-cream scooper filled with tiny mints or gourmet jellybeans. Make sure each favor has a tag or ribbon to mark the day.

Adopt-a-Bride

Suggestions

Identify the Bride: Decide who you plan to assist with her wedding. Reach out to friends, community organizations, and local churches. In most churches, the clerk will include this kind of service in the weekly bulletin or announcements. If there is a want-ad board at church, be sure to hang up a poster and include an e-mail address or your telephone number at work. Don't give out your home number to strangers.

Talent: Let the bride know about your talent. Our community is very diverse—beauticians, makeup artists, caterers, singers, desktop publishers, writers, seamstresses, decorators. Whatever it is that you can do will help her. Your talent might be fast envelope stuffer or calligrapher.

Arrangements: Set up a meeting to discuss the when, the where, and the how. Be very specific, punctual, and reliable. Stay in close contact with the bride so that she will not be nervous about you leaving her hanging.

Requests: Find out if she needs anything specific or if she has any wishes or ideas that she would like fulfilled. If she seems a little shy, tell her to give you a wish list. You may know another girlfriend who can help the bride.

Extras: Recycle your wedding gown. Perhaps there is a bride who wants to look like Cinderella on her big day but can't afford it. If she looks about your size, offer to let her wear your gown on her magical day. More women are opting to wear secondhand dresses instead of spending thousands. If she insists on something new, then help her locate discount stores.

Christmas in July Barbecue

Menu #1
Grilled Chicken, Shrimp, & Filet Mignon
Baked Potato
Corn on the Cob
Ginger Veggie Salad
Dinner Rolls
Christmas Cookies
Punch

Menu #2
Barbecued Spare Ribs & Chicken
Macaroni Salad
Baked Beans
Garden Salad
Corn Bread
Strawberry Cheesecake
Strawberry Daiquiris

Menu #3
Hamburgers
Hot Dogs
Turkey Hero Sandwiches
Potato Salad
Grilled Veggies
Carrot Cake
Frozen Margaritas

Suggestions

Host: A group of girlfriends can give this event together or one girlfriend can host it alone. You decide what works best for you.

Invitations: Buy Christmas party invitations at the end of the holiday season. You'll be sure to catch a good sale. If you want to really get creative, design a personalized invitation on your home computer. When your guests receive these invitations in the mail, your telephone is sure to ring. Ask each guest to bring an unwrapped toy, book, or gift for a child. Mail three weeks in advance.

Attire: All guests should be required to wear something red in order to get into the barbecue. Give a gift to the person who has on the most red.

Donations: Let your guests know who their gifts will be given to. One idea is to include this information on the invitation or make an announcement at the party. Do not turn down monetary gifts. Be sure to make sure these donations are checks written out to the organization or family you plan to help.

Decorations: Go all out, girlfriend! That's right, pull out the artificial tree and all the trimmings. Don't think about cleaning up. Your wonderful girlfriends will be there to lend a helping hand. Use Christmas lights to brighten the yard when the sun goes down. Deck the holly all over the joint. Christmas toilet paper, paper towels, and serving trays add a nice touch. Use red, green, silver, and gold balloons to decorate. Get a Christmas tablecloth and paper and plastic goods.

Music: No matter how badly your girlfriends want you to change the music, only play Christmas tunes except for the electric slide. You'll be surprised how many of your favorite groups have Christmas CDs. One of my favorites is Boys II Men. I also picked up a great Calypso Christmas tape while in the Bahamas—it's wonderful. Be creative—start collecting Christmas music in advance. You'll need at least six hours of music to keep the party going

Entertainment: Get Santa to make a guest appearance at your party. He can pass out candy canes and favors to your guests in the middle of the party. If you decide to invite children to your party, they will get a kick out of seeing Santa. Call your local costume shop or party service company to get old St. Nick off the beach and into his red suit for the day. To raise extra money for your charity or family, charge everyone a dollar or two to have their picture taken with Santa (make sure you have a Polaroid and lots of film).

Favors: Remember, a little memento is always nice to mark the day. Whether you decide to give a small box of chocolates, a bundle of homemade Christmas cookies, or a T-shirt with "Just Between Girlfriends Christmas in July Barbecue," be sure to wrap or ribbon the gift. Make it look like a Christmas gift.

Back-to-the-Beach Party

Suggestions

Invitation: Send each of your girlfriends a small inflatable float, beach ball, or toy with a note telling them to meet you at the beach. If you have the time, hand write the note so that it will appear to be a more personal invitation. Put the inflatable toy in the envelope and mail it. Mail it at least a month in advance so that the date will not conflict with summer vacations.

Beach Stuff: Bathing suit, sunglasses, towel, suntan lotion or sunscreen, beach ball, frisbee, volleyball set, binoculars, pail and shovel, camera, your child's boom box, your favorite CDs and tapes, deck of cards, video camera, beach chair, and your favorite novel.

Picnic Basket: Don't bother cooking. Just stop off and get a bucket of chicken, a couple of hero sandwiches (hold the mayo—bring a small jar), and keep everything in a cooler. Make a salad and some of Dottie's macaroni salad. Get plenty of chips, popcorn, pretzels, candy, and your favorite beverages.

Mission: Enjoy a grown-up day at the beach without trying to locate lost children or worrying that you will not get a moment of peace.

African-American Girlfriend Beauties

Invitation: No need to send out invitations. Pick a date before saying good-bye to your girlfriends at the beach. A Saturday would probably be the best day for this activity because it requires a full day.

Shopping: All girlfriends know how to shop, but not all girlfriends know where to find a good sale. Looking good doesn't always mean spending your whole check. There are ways to purchase designer dresses and good-quality clothing for a fraction of the cost. Check the sale racks. It's also possible that you might have something you want to wear in your closet.

Appointment: Book appointments at the spa or pampering palace in advance. Whenever there is a party of five or more, some salons have a hard time accommodating them. When you make appointments, be sure to let the receptionist know you are a group. Ask if they have a facility for you to get dressed there. Ask for a brochure.

Services: Be specific about what you want. While some places have package deals, the services at most spas are á la carte. Get a price list so that there will be no surprises! If you have a favorite shampoo, nail polish color, or fragrance, take it with you.

Stuff to Bring: A camera and lots of film, video camera and someone who is willing to operate it, and an open mind. Be daring! Let the spa give you a new edge, whether it's a haircut, arched eyebrows, or makeup tips. Go for it! Get a makeover.

Restaurant Reservations: Call early. Let the restaurant know it will be a large party.

Men: If you decide to bring the men, let them know you'll be spending the entire day getting dolled up for them. Hopefully, they will get a haircut and shave in honor of the day.

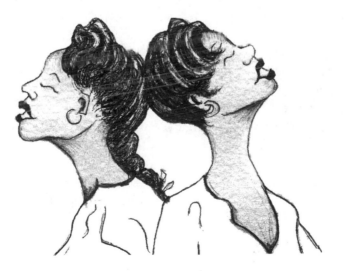

Girlfriends' Getaway Weekend

Where: Bermuda, Bahamas, or the Cayman Islands! It doesn't matter where you go, just go somewhere over a three-day weekend. Call Grandma and Grandpa, if they live close by, and ask them to take care of the kids while you enjoy a little fun in the sun with your girlfriends.

When: My girlfriends and I have made a pact to spend every Columbus Day weekend together. Our first annual Just Between Girlfriends' Getaway Weekend will be to Nassau, Bahamas. Come on and join us; it's going to be a blast. Drop us a line for more details.

Stuff to Pack: At least two bathing suits, cover-up (if your thighs are as big as mine), shades, and a couple of light-weight outfits. Don't overpack; you don't need a lot of clothes when you're on vacation. But I do suggest a few cute little numbers. Oooh yeah—bring the binoculars, girlfriend! Hey, you never know.

Mission: Fun, Fun, Fun! Don't bother bringing a book to read on this trip because we'll be too busy having a blast.

Pin the Tail on the Turkey

Invitations: Spread your five fingers out on a sheet of paper, just like when you were a kid, and trace them. Cut this out and wha-la—you have a turkey invitation. Be sure to list the time, day, date, and place. Include a note or letter telling each woman to bring a picture of her turkey(s). Feel free to explain the game ahead of time or go for the element of surprise—it's up to you.

Nosh: Call out for Chinese, pizza, or something quick and easy. If you think your girlfriends have time to get into the kitchen, you could make this event pot luck—you decide.

Music: None of those old love tunes. Not tonight, girlfriend. Pull out some party sounds that will make you want to shake, shake, shake your booty.

Favors: They may not walk out the door with this favor, but whenever they get it you know they'll smile. I think a picture of your girlfriend pinning the tail on the turkey to document the night would be hilarious. To keep the cost down, use the same finger-traced turkey idea and attach the picture. If you can, laminate and frame each one before you send it out.

to get a little closer to your sweetie, then go ahead and play a little Luther Vandross.

Favors: Okay, this is going to be a challenge, but try to make a calendar for the New Year that contains pictures of you and your girlfriends. Use the pictures you've taken throughout the year. They will be shocked! This can be done on your personal computer or by using a pen, ruler, and paper—then make copies and bind with ribbon.

Stories, Stories, Stories!

ALL GIRLFRIENDS HAVE THEM. IF YOU ARE INTERESTED IN sharing a heartwarming, unusual, or hilarious story about you and your girlfriends, type it (two-page limit) and mail it to me at the address below. Include your name, address, and telephone number so that I can contact you in the event that your story is selected for new editions of the book or *Just Between Girlfriends Newsletter*.

Just Between Girlfriends Newsletter

Would you like to connect with other Just Between Girlfriends readers? Receive a free "Girlfriends" appreciation gift? Do you want more information about book signings in your area, a Web site, recipes, and events such as our upcoming Just Between Girlfriends' Getaway Weekend trip or our Mother's Day Fashion Show? All this and more can be found in the Just Between Girlfriends Newsletter. Send a self-addressed, stamped (letter-size) envelope, your business card or typed label with your name, address, and telephone number, and a $5 check or money order payable to:

Just Between Girlfriends Newsletter
P.O. Box 7126
Rochelle Park, New Jersey 07662-9998

Also, feel free to send comments about *Just Between Girlfriends*. Thank you for your support, girlfriends!

About the Author

Chrisena Coleman is an award-winning journalist at the New York *Daily News* and the author of *Mama Knows Best: African-American Wives' Tales, Myths, and Remedies for Mothers and Mothers-to-Be*. Coleman has written for *Essence, Emerge,* and *BET Weekend* magazines. She frequently guest-hosts *Night Talk* (the country's only nationally syndicated African-American radio talk show). She also does a weekly news commentary segment for WWRL-AM radio in New York. She lives in Hackensack, New Jersey, with her three-year-old son, Jordan.